AFFIrMpress

Elise Bialylew is the founder of Mindful in May, an online global mindfulness campaign that teaches thousands of people each year to meditate, while raising funds to build clean water projects in the developing world. A doctor trained in psychiatry, turned social entrepreneur, she's passionate about supporting individuals and organisations to develop inner tools for greater wellbeing and flourishing. She offers workshops and corporate training at The Mind Life Project. Her work has featured in the *Huffington Post, New York Times,* and on Australian television.

www.mindfulinmay.org
www.mindlifeproject.com

the
happiness
plan

the
happiness
plan

A one-month mindfulness guide to
reduce stress, improve wellbeing
and transform your life.

by Dr Elise Bialylew

Published by Affirm Press in 2018
28 Thistlethwaite Street, South Melbourne, VIC 3205.
www.affirmpress.com.au

National Library of Australia Cataloguing-in-Publication entry available
for this title at www.nla.gov.au

Title: The Happiness Plan / Elise Bialylew, author.
ISBN: 9781925584769 (paperback)

Cover Design: Christa Moffitt, Christabella Design
Cover photograph: Fi Mims, fimimsphotography.com.au
Internal design by Christa Moffitt, Christabella Design, and Maegan Brown
Typesetting by J&M Typesetting
Proudly printed in Australia by Griffin Press

The paper this book is printed on is certified against the Forest Stewardship
Council* Standards. Griffin Press holds FSC chain of custody certification
SGS-COC-005088. FSC promotes environmentally responsible, socially
beneficial and economically viable management of the world's forests.

All reasonable effort has been made to attribute copyright and credit. Any
new information supplied will be included in subsequent editions.

CONTENTS

*To my parents, who have enriched my life
with their boundless generosity and love.*

'If you begin to understand what you are without
trying to change it, then what you are
undergoes a transformation.'
J Krishnamurti

'I don't have to chase extraordinary moments
to find happiness — it's right in front of me if I'm paying
attention and practising gratitude.'
Brené Brown

Introduction

Few experiences can compare to holding a human brain.

It was my first year of medical training. I was nineteen years old, and as I stood in the cold, sterile dissection room with a brain in my hands, I wondered how a lifetime of memory, feelings and thoughts could arise from this one-kilogram tofu-like substance. This fascination with the brain, coupled with my desire to help people live happy and meaningful lives, led me to a career in psychiatry.

As I moved deeper into my career I discovered that while psychiatry helped save people's lives, it often left the flourishing part of the equation to other health professionals. I also realised that this was the part of the journey I was most passionate about. I wanted to support people in thriving, not just surviving.

Truth be told, throughout my training, as I worked twenty-four-hour shifts on the wards, my own health and happiness were being affected. As a highly sensitive person who deeply cared about her fellow human beings, the work I was doing was taking its toll, at times leaving me stressed and overwhelmed.

I wasn't alone. As I spoke with my colleagues, I discovered a silent epidemic of doctors experiencing vicarious trauma, compassion fatigue and existential crises of their own. One day I turned up to work to find that one colleague had admitted himself to a psychiatric clinic. The pressure had sent him spiralling into a severe depression.

I knew I wanted to be of service, to help others flourish and make a positive difference in the world, but I sensed I wasn't moving in the right direction. I valued the rigour of science and the solid foundation of knowledge my training gave me, but I was feeling unfulfilled and confused. I knew I wasn't on the right path, but I wasn't sure how to course correct.

The words of writer Rainer Maria Rilke were a great consolation at this time:

Be patient toward all that is unsolved in your heart and try to love the questions themselves, like locked rooms and like books that are written in a very foreign tongue. Do not now seek the answers, which cannot be given you because you would not be able to live them. And the point is, to live everything. Live the questions now. Perhaps you will then gradually, without noticing it, live along some distant day into the answer.

And live into the answer I did.

If you've picked up this book, I'm guessing that you are also curious about how to experience greater happiness in your life. Perhaps you're looking for ways to reduce stress and feel calmer, or maybe you're going through a transition that's causing suffering in your life: a relationship breakup, career dissatisfaction or a recent health issue. Or perhaps you're a seeker and lifelong learner who thrives on discovering the latest science to support you in living your best life.

You've come to the right place.

It was during my own search for clarity, happiness and resilience that I discovered mindfulness meditation.

It was the early 2000s, and mindfulness had not yet hit the mainstream medical world. I attended a conference and heard leading neuroscientists Dr Richard Davidson and Dr Michael Merzenich talk about the impact of mindfulness on the brain, and the new science of neuroplasticity – the brain's capacity to adapt and change throughout our lifetime in response to our experiences.

I was intrigued. Only a few years earlier, the accepted view in science was that the brain rapidly developed until about our mid-twenties, at which point brain-cell growth stopped and our capacity to create new neural pathways significantly reduced. It was a depressing picture of our brain's capacity, peaking early and then declining into old age. But by the time of the conference, Davidson and a few other leaders in the field of neuroscience were correcting this misconception. A new understanding of the brain was emerging, and it provided much more exciting possibilities.

Davidson shared research demonstrating that mental training such as meditation actually changed meditators' brains – both functionally *and* structurally – in ways that supported greater happiness and wellbeing. The changes were even seen in relatively short periods of meditation practice: one of Davidson's studies revealed that just seven hours of compassion meditation over a two-week period resulted in measurable changes in the brain, and also had a positive impact on behaviour, leading to increased altruism. Meanwhile, in a study of rats, Merzenich and his team demonstrated that regular brain training not only allowed their brains to continue growing and maintain function into old age, but could actually *reverse* age-related functional decline. His later studies found the same outcomes for humans who participated in intense brain training. The lifelong potential of neuroplasticity was emerging as a crucial element of our collective scientific understanding, empowering us to reach optimal levels of wellbeing.

These scientists were suggesting that just as practising an instrument improves one's musical abilities, implementing regular mind and brain practices could improve our psychological and physical wellbeing. I realised this perspective on wellbeing could offer hope to my patients, many of whom believed that their potential for happiness was limited by their genetics. Many saw themselves destined to a fate of familial anxiety or depression, with no capacity to influence this trajectory.

Although genetics undeniably has an influence on our mental health, the new science offered a more empowering perspective, where we could, to some extent, become sculptors of our own brains.

I realised that I was witnessing a paradigm shift in the world of wellbeing. Old models were being shattered as new models emerged, revealing the undiscovered potential of our brains. Scientific research was supporting what Buddhist monks had known for well over two thousand years: that meditation was a powerful tool for enhancing wellbeing, clarity and happiness.

As I continued to explore this robust science, I was inspired to do my own investigation into mindfulness and the brain, so I dived head-first into meditation by signing up for a seven-day silent meditation retreat.

My psychiatry boss at the time warned me against it. 'I had a patient who lost their mind on one of those things. I couldn't think of anything worse,' he casually remarked.

To be honest, I was a little scared too. Spending a week in silence with only my mind as company terrified me. As a high-energy person who likes to be productive and creative, I didn't consider myself the ideal candidate for meditation. However, despite my reservations, a few weeks later I found myself on a meditation cushion in a retreat centre in the Byron Bay Hinterland.

During the first few days I struggled. I was falling asleep from boredom and exhaustion in some moments, then experiencing the most profound levels of agitation at others. It felt like an army of ants was crawling under my skin.

Then, after three days of obsessively questioning what I was doing there and contemplating escape plans, an unfamiliar sense of calm emerged. It was as though I'd been living my whole life with a background of mental static, and suddenly it cleared. I felt strangely content being right where I was, even though what I was doing was objectively pretty boring.

On the afternoon of the fourth day I strolled around the retreat grounds, strangely captivated by the details of trees and plants. Colourful flowers seemed more vibrant, leaf patterns and shapes were as fascinating as works of art, the melodic bird song as thrilling as a live music concert. I was completely present, absorbed in the moment. The narrating, planning, judging, worrying voice in my head had disappeared. There was stillness, ease and a feeling of deep connection to everything.

I laughed at my clichéd transformation. I'd quickly gone from being a driven, ambitious, latte-sipping, list-making city dweller, to a bird-watching, contemplative, calm, nature-admiring meditator. After only a few days of silent practice I had indeed 'lost my mind', but in the most positive way.

When I arrived home from the retreat, my partner noticed the difference too. He told me I seemed calmer and more present.

I didn't realise it at the time, but this turning inwards was the beginning of a profound shift in the direction of my life.

As I continued training in mindfulness with some of the world's leading teachers, I was inspired by the qualities they embodied: wisdom, happiness, humility, generosity, patience, and compassion. However, although I knew how powerful this training was, I felt confused about how to share it in the mainstream setting of a psychiatry ward. At the time it felt too far off the beaten track. At a training retreat I attended with Jon Kabat-Zinn, one of the early pioneers of mindfulness in the West, I shared my confusion about how I could use what I was practising in the context of my psychiatry training.

'I've been training in psychiatry, but I feel like something has been missing in its model of wellbeing. I've experienced the power of mindfulness in my own life and I know there's solid science to back it, but I don't know how to get past the cynicism and resistance to it in the medical world. How do I convince other doctors that it's not too esoteric?'

Jon answered compassionately: 'Do you know what aikido is?'

'I know it's a type of martial art,' I replied.

'It's a martial art that works gracefully with the energy of another, rather than against it. You need to do aikido with the system.'

I must have looked puzzled, because he elaborated, suggesting that I gently bring mindfulness into the system, experimenting with different ways to integrate it into my work.

At that moment I realised it was my own limited beliefs about the medical world that were holding me back. The answer lay in finding whatever small doorways would allow me to share what I had learned.

Not long after my training with Jon Kabat-Zinn, a groundbreaking study emerged supporting the impact mindfulness could have on mental health, specifically depression. A group of psychologists in England named Mark Williams, John Teasdale and Zindel Segal conducted a study of patients who had suffered multiple episodes of depression. Incredibly, they found that mindfulness practice was at least as effective in preventing depressive relapse as maintenance antidepressants – without any of the side effects. A later study building on this discovery found that mindfulness practice could nearly halve the risk of depressive relapse.

This research impressed even the most biologically minded psychiatrists. Following this research, one psychiatric clinic began running pilot mindfulness programs, which I co-facilitated, for people with anxiety, depression and addiction. I remember one woman in her sixties, a recovering alcoholic who had a volatile relationship with her daughter. She found that mindfulness opened her up to vital new ways of communicating. At the completion of the two-month program she shared that she'd had a powerful conversation with her daughter that led to tears of sadness and joy. They'd felt a mutual connection, something they hadn't experienced for decades.

Another participant, who had suffered chronic depression and who had tried multiple medications with no sustained improvement, reluctantly arrived at the group following his psychologist's referral. He was cynical, impatient and at times quite agitated that nothing was changing. He'd get lost in doubts and stuck with the hopeless, helpless lens that tinted his reality. I was surprised each week to see him return, sure that he was going to drop out. At some level, I started to wonder whether mindfulness really could help him. In those moments

I remembered some of Jon Kabat-Zinn's advice: 'You need to let go of any attachment to needing something to happen for your participants. Just be patient and trust the process.'

As we approached the end of the program, the man started to have more frequent insights, which slowly coalesced towards a deeper shift. He shared his learnings with the group, explaining that he'd discovered he could watch his thoughts rather than believe all of them: 'I've learned how to be kinder to myself rather than being such a critical bastard all the time.' He went on to describe how mindfulness was helping him catch himself when he began falling into depressive rumination and helped him redirect his attention away from the mental quicksand, and back to the breath or sounds around him. Most profoundly, mindfulness was helping him notice all the things he actually had in his life, including his wife and loving daughters, even in the midst of his depression.

A doorway to greater happiness and purpose

Many people in the West have been drawn to meditation or mindfulness with the hope of finding better ways to manage their stress. However, although these practices can be a powerful antidote to the stress in our lives, they have a much deeper capacity to transform us.

There are so many books that boast magical, quick fixes to life's challenges, and judging by the number that are hitting the bestseller lists, it seems that many of us are searching for that 'secret' to achieving lasting happiness. We are obsessed with trying to avoid the suffering that comes with being human.

In our relentless pursuit of happiness, we can easily get caught running on 'the hedonic treadmill', constantly seeking external sources of pleasure. Whether it's earning more money, finding the 'perfect' relationship, or seeking approval, power, or success, we look for happiness in areas that are often transient and outside of our control. Our desires just keep bubbling up as we struggle to fill the gap between our current reality and some imagined better reality 'over there'.

But there is another form of wellbeing and happiness, called eudaimonic happiness, first explored by Aristotle several thousand years ago. Eudaimonia comes from two Greek words: *eu*, meaning 'good', and *Daimon*, which is translated as 'soul' or 'self'. This type of flourishing is not dependent on external circumstances, but rather emerges from an inner sense of wellbeing; it's created by what we bring to life rather than what we get out of it, and it is completely within our control. Mindfulness training connects us to our inner reservoir of wellbeing, and helps us see the causes of our happiness and suffering. With this growing wisdom and clarity, we make better decisions and start to experience a happiness that transcends our never-ending flow of wanting.

Don't get me wrong, I love life's pleasures – whether it's eating a delicious meal, hearing live music, dancing or travelling somewhere new. However, over time I've begun to recognise how fleeting these things are and how insatiable my appetite for pleasure can be.

The good news is that this book is a guide to experiencing more eudaimonia – or genuine happiness – in your life. And there's no bad news, other than it will take some time each day to master the skill.

I'm not going to teach you magical ways to 'manifest anything you want' or solutions to eliminating life's inevitable challenges (although I wish I could). This book won't help you find your 'perfect soulmate' or 'get rich quick'. However, you will discover a completely new way of understanding your thoughts and mind that, as far as I've found, is the real 'secret' to supporting your greatest happiness.

When I started learning mindfulness meditation I had no idea how deeply it would transform my life. One morning, when I had been meditating for several years and was almost at the end of my psychiatry training, I was sitting in meditation when a phrase appeared in my mind, flashing like a neon light: 'Mindful in May'. The phrase grew into an idea to create an online global month of mindfulness each year during May, where people could be taught about mindfulness by leading experts from around the world and dedicate the month to making a positive difference by raising funds for global poverty.

This was the beginning of a new path that would answer the call of my longing to make a positive difference in a more far-reaching way than prescribing medication and facilitating small group meetings. It was an idea that integrated three of my passions: mindfulness, social impact and community building through technology.

Over the weeks that followed, I sat with the idea and let it simmer in my mind. Although I was passionate about it, I began to doubt whether I had the skills and capacity to make it happen, grappling with thoughts such as, 'How am I going to run an online campaign with absolutely no tech knowledge?' I had become so conditioned to the hierarchy of the medical world that it felt completely new to take a leap without a senior colleague giving me the go ahead. I had spent my whole life carefully studying before I took action, and now I was going to have to take action first and learn along the way.

At this time, I stumbled across a book called *The War of Art* by Steven Pressfield, which explored the phenomenon of resistance. Pressfield wrote:

Resistance can show up in many forms and often it's through self-criticism or self-doubt. Here's the mistake we make when we listen to the voice of self-doubt: We misperceive a force that is universal and impersonal and instead see it as individual and personal. That voice in our heads is not us. It is Resistance ... To yield to resistance deforms our spirit. It stunts us and makes us less than we are and were born to be.

His words, together with an impending deadline of May, pushed me into action. I took the plunge and started to bring the vision to life.

Since its creation, Mindful in May has taught thousands of people from more than thirty-five countries how to meditate, while at the same time bringing better health to those in the developing world. It has brought contentment, joy and connection to those in the developed world by teaching the skills of mindfulness, and at the same time has saved lives in the developing world by raising money to build clean water wells in Africa. Corporate organisations including Google, as well as schools, government, and high-profile Australian individuals, have become champions of Mindful in May. Participants who complete the program almost universally report an improvement in mental clarity, reduction in stress and an increased appreciation of daily life.

Much of the research in the field of mindfulness explores the impact of thirty to forty-five minutes of meditation a day on physical and psychological wellbeing. However, since the inception of the Mindful in May program I noticed that the participants were reporting the benefits of just ten minutes' daily practice. This led me to investigate through a research study whether ten minutes of meditation a day over one month had any tangible benefits. Excitingly, the study, which included over two hundred people from the program, suggested exactly what we'd suspected. Ten minutes of mindfulness meditation a day over one month was enough to support more positive emotions, reduce stress, increase self-compassion and strengthen focus in daily life.

HOW TEN MINUTES OF MEDITATION FOR ONE MONTH DURING **MINDFUL IN MAY** AFFECTED PARTICIPANTS

'I am prone to shocking anxiety and meditation has really helped with that. I just passed my three-hundred-day mark since I started meditating regularly with Mindful in May. That really kickstarted it for me – consistency has always been my problem. Being guided through Mindful in May to meditate for ten minutes is very doable in this busy life, and you still get the benefits.'
– Magda Szubanski, actor, comedian and writer

'I confess I was a cynic about meditation and mindfulness. But after my husband died suddenly in 2014, and I was confronted with night after night of terrible insomnia, a friend suggested I give Mindful in May a go and I thought, "What have I got to lose in committing ten minutes a day to something?" My sleep improved, symptoms of a chronic physical health condition improved and I felt more alert and capable to deal with the craziness of everyday life. By bringing mindfulness into my daily routine, I have seen significant improvements in my overall wellbeing.'

– Fiona Grinwald, writer and founder of 2lookup

The benefits and applications of mindfulness

Although it may seem like mindfulness is a recent trend, it actually originated from Buddhist contemplative practices that are over 2500 years old. The original word for mindfulness in the Pali language of the ancient Buddhist texts is *sati*. This has a number of different meanings, including 'to familiarise' or 'to remember'. Mindfulness training familiarises us with the nature of the mind, helping us to recognise more clearly what leads to suffering and what leads to happiness. The training sharpens our ability to 'remember' to return to the present moment, especially when we get lost in unhelpful thinking – the kind that unnecessarily amplifies our stress, entangling us in worries about things that usually don't end up happening.

Many other definitions of mindfulness have emerged over time, but in essence, it is …

… a clear, curious and present–moment awareness of what is happening within us and around us, from moment to moment.

In the 1970s Jon Kabat-Zinn was the first to explore the benefits of mindfulness in a mainstream context by bringing it into the hospital setting. He wanted to explore whether it could reduce the suffering of those with complex medical illnesses and pain. He discovered that mindfulness training had powerful, measurable effects not only on the minds but also on the bodies of people with various health conditions. Some of Kabat-Zinn's earliest research in 1998, conducted through his program Mindfulness-Based Stress Reduction (MBSR), found that patients suffering from psoriasis (a chronic skin condition) who participated in mindfulness programs healed more rapidly than the group that received conventional treatment alone. His research also explored the benefits of mindfulness for those suffering chronic pain, revealing significant improvements in the quality of life for patients not only during the program, but also in the longer term. Impressively, these 225 patients were followed over a four-year period and a majority of them were still experiencing the benefits with a sustained mindfulness practice.

In her book *The How of Happiness*, Sonja Lyubomirsky, one of the world's leading researchers in positive psychology, reveals that although up to fifty per cent of our potential happiness is determined by our genetic makeup and ten per cent by life circumstances that are out of our control, forty per cent of our potential happiness *is* within our control and determined by 'what we do in our daily lives and how we think'.

Moreover, studies in the field of epigenetics demonstrate that it's not simply the genes we inherit that determine our destinies. The way in which they are expressed also has a powerful impact on our wellbeing, ranging from our risk of getting cancer to whether we will be overweight or suffer from depression. We now know that our environment and lifestyle choices (including our diet, exercise and stress levels) can have a profound impact on which genes are turned on or off.

Excitingly, research also shows that mindfulness meditation can positively impact on the way certain genes are expressed. In one of the most groundbreaking studies to date, Richard Davidson demonstrated that just one day of mindfulness practice could reduce the expression of specific genes associated with inflammation in the body, a known risk factor for various chronic illnesses. This discovery has spiked the interest of even the most sceptical scientists.

During my training as a doctor, the mind and body were often considered separate entities. Research like Davidson's has forced us to completely rethink this concept. The discovery that a form of mental training can influence the body right down to the level of our genetic expression is extraordinary, and highlights the intimate connection between our mind and body. It is helping dissolve the artificial boundaries that have been drawn between body and mind for centuries. We are finally understanding that it would be more accurate to consider ourselves a 'body–mind' – one integrated whole.

With the World Health Organisation (WHO) announcing that depression has become the leading cause of ill health and disability worldwide, we must learn how to manage the increasing stress of life. Mindfulness is one skill that can strengthen our inner resources to better cope with the inevitable demands of being human. More than just 'nice to have', it's become an essential life skill that we need to help us navigate these increasingly complex times.

MINDFULNESS VS. MEDITATION: WHAT IS THE DIFFERENCE?

The words 'mindfulness' and 'meditation' are often used interchangeably, but there is a difference between them. In the simplest terms, mindfulness is a form of meditation. 'Meditation' can be used to describe any discipline that involves training your mind to reduce suffering. There are many different forms of meditation originating from different philosophies, including transcendental, tantric and creative visualisation meditation – and of course mindfulness meditation. In other words, meditation describes a collection of different forms of mental training that ultimately lead to the same place: greater clarity, wisdom and happiness in life.

With so many different options how do you know which one to choose? As a doctor trained in psychiatry, I was drawn to mindfulness meditation because it can be practised in a completely secular way, is not attached to any particular religion or culture, and has the greatest number of evidence-based benefits. But rather than trusting me blindly, I suggest that you practise mindfulness meditation every day this month and see what benefits you experience.

Understanding the mind and building resilience

As humans we have a unique evolutionary advantage, with minds that can project into the future, solve complex problems and generate creative ideas that transform what is possible. However, this unique talent comes at a cost. With minds that are free to time travel between past, present and future, we get excessively caught up in future thinking that creates unnecessary worry in our lives.

HOW MINDFUL ARE YOU?

You can do a quick test right now to see how mindful you are. Remember that you can't fail this experiment; it's a quick way for you to see that, just like everyone else, your mind gets easily distracted.

Allow yourself to sit or lie comfortably. Close your eyes and feel your breath moving in and out of your body. Then, at the end of each outbreath, begin to count. See how many breaths you can count silently to yourself without getting distracted and losing track of the number.

Try it out now and come back to this passage when you've given it a go.

Remember the number that you counted before getting distracted, write it down somewhere, and at the end of this month of mindfulness, do the test again and see what number you can get up to after a month of mental training!

If you tried this experiment, you may have noticed how easy it is to get distracted and lose track of the count. Most of the time there is a constant stream of thoughts running through our minds, though we are not always aware of it. It affects our capacity to be present, and unconsciously influences our behaviours and decisions.

Maybe you can relate to the experience of sitting down to work and catching yourself jumping between tasks, feeling like you're not really doing anything properly. Or perhaps you've noticed how easily you can get hijacked by your Facebook stream and waste hours numbing out when you could have spent that time doing something far more productive (like meditating!). Maybe you're finding it difficult to switch off and go to sleep at night because your mind is racing through all the things you need to do the next day.

The truth is, we often have very little control over our thoughts; in many ways, our mind has a mind of its own. The untrained mind jumps from thought to thought, like a monkey jumping from branch to branch. In mindfulness meditation training, this is referred to as 'the monkey mind'.

In a famous study, Daniel Gilbert, an American psychologist, aimed to investigate just how distracted our minds actually are, and what impact this has on our overall happiness. Participants were asked three questions at random times throughout the day: 'What are you doing?', 'Where is your attention?' and 'What's your mood like?' Gilbert found that people were distracted about forty-seven per cent of the time, but even more interestingly, he found a strong correlation between having a distracted mind and feeling stressed and unhappy. When people were not focused on what they were doing, regardless of the type of activity, they described feeling less happy. The conclusion of the study was that a wandering mind is an unhappy mind.

One of the fascinating things about our mind is that thoughts can be voluntary or involuntary. While we can actively bring a thought to mind, many just arise of their own accord, and it's the unprompted negative thoughts that get us all tangled up and stressed out. When a negative thought comes to mind our natural tendency is to push it away. Paradoxically, this only amplifies the thought. In 1863, Russian novelist and philosopher Fyodor Dostoyevsky was considering the problem: 'Try to pose for yourself this task: not to think of a polar bear, and you will see that the cursed thing will come to mind every minute.' We can choose to bring a thought up, but we can't stop it from arising, and when we try to deliberately suppress a thought, it makes it more likely to appear.

Just like the breath, which continuously flows in and out without needing our awareness or control (luckily!), the thought stream is for the most part an involuntary flow. Although we can't completely control what thoughts will come to mind, we can choose how we relate to them, and this is life-changing. The capacity to better manage our minds and avoid getting lost in negative thought loops is a crucial skill that helps us become more resilient, better able to bounce back from challenges and not get stuck in negative thinking and emotions. Richard Davidson, who featured as one of the many experts in the Mindful in May campaign, shared his perspectives on the relationship between mindfulness and resilience:

Through regular mindfulness meditation we have discovered that there are certain changes in the brain that are associated with decreased stickiness. By stickiness, we're referring to a propensity to ruminate on or to stew in our negative emotions. When adversity happens it's appropriate and adaptive to experience whatever negative emotions may arise, but then to let them go when they're no longer useful. Meditation can help to facilitate that.

Just as our immune system protects us from toxic bacteria and viruses, regular mindfulness practice protects us from unhelpful thinking and rumination by helping us develop awareness of what is happening in our minds. With this enhanced clarity and awareness we become masters, rather than the slaves of our minds.

Davidson's research also gave us insight into the connection between two crucial brain regions involved in regulating emotion, namely the amygdala and the prefrontal cortex. The amygdala – or fear centre of the brain – is part of the 'old brain', designed to bypass the thinking brain so that our responses to danger are immediate and don't rely on the more time-consuming thinking process. Fortunately, our brains also evolved to house the prefrontal cortex, located behind the forehead and responsible for many of our uniquely human capacities such as using language, focusing attention, making decisions and managing our emotions. The prefrontal cortex can significantly reduce the intensity of the amygdala's activation, helping us calm ourselves down when we've been emotionally triggered. This works very much like a wise, compassionate mother (the prefrontal cortex) soothing an upset child (the amygdala).

Davidson's research in this area demonstrated that people who meditated for a minimum of thirty hours over two months had less active amygdalas, meaning less propensity to be stressed. Furthermore, in expert meditators the connection between the amygdala and the prefrontal cortex increased, leading to an improved ability to calm down when under emotional stress, supporting resilience.

We are only just beginning to understand the potential impact that meditation can have on the brain, but what is clear is that mindfulness, when practiced regularly, can lead to long-lasting transformation. This form of mental training can not only support us in experiencing more positive short-lived 'states' of being, such as feeling increased calm or more focus, but more profoundly, it can transform our 'traits' – the enduring patterns of our personalities.

The evidence of this finding has largely come from neuroscientists who investigated the brains of expert meditators – those who have spent thousands of hours in meditation. Over the past decade, the scientists at Richard Davidson's lab have been studying the brain of Mingyur Rinpoche, a Tibetan monk who has spent many years in intensive meditation retreats, and what they discovered was completely unprecedented.

You may have heard of the term 'brain waves': these are the electrical patterns created when a group of neurons (brain cells) communicate with each other. Our brains release different waves depending on what we are doing with them, and these waves are measured and recorded by a machine called an EEG.

There are four main types of EEG patterns that correspond to different activities in the brain. In simplified terms, the slower brain waves are associated with slower mental states, such as sleep or tiredness, while the faster brain waves are associated with alertness and concentration. While we are in deep sleep the brain shows mainly delta waves (the slowest waves), when we're drowsy or in a daydreaming mode the brain shows mainly theta waves (the next slowest), while we're not doing anything in particular the brain shows alpha waves, and while we're concentrating on a task or thinking, the brain shows beta waves (which are fastest). There is another type of brain wave that is the very fastest of all, and which happens when we have a moment of insight and our brain regions all activate together: gamma waves. Increased gamma waves are associated with heightened sensory perception, memory recall, focus, and even compassion and calm. They are signs of a brain functioning at its peak. In most people these gamma waves only ever happen in a flash lasting a few seconds at most, but Rinpoche's brain, and those of other expert meditators, showed a pattern of gamma waves lasting for minutes.

In *The Science of Meditation*, Daniel Goleman explains:

No brain lab had ever before seen gamma oscillations that persist for minutes rather than split seconds, are so strong, and are in synchrony across widespread regions of the brain. Astonishingly, this sustained, brain-entraining gamma pattern goes on even while seasoned meditators are asleep … These gamma oscillations continuing during deep sleep are, again, something never seen before and seem to reflect a residual quality of awareness that persists day and night. For the first time, Davidson and fellow researcher Antoine Lutz were seeing a neural echo of the enduring transformations that years of meditation practice etch onto the brain.

Although most of us will not complete years of solo meditation like Mingyur Rinpoche, these findings provide us with a new perspective on what may be possible through a committed meditation practice. Just as we gain deep insight into the universe through the perspective of astronauts who return from outer space and share their discoveries, those who dedicate so many years to investigating the nature of the mind offer us deeper understandings of our own inner universe. And just as Olympic athletes demonstrate the extraordinary potential of the human body when rigorously trained, we too can be inspired by the discoveries of these Olympic meditators, who reveal the potential of our own minds.

Experiencing our greatest potential for happiness involves a commitment to both our bodies and our minds. The importance of physical exercise in supporting our wellbeing is well understood within our society, but for too long we have failed to place the same emphasis on mental exercise.

Our mind is our most precious resource. It's the source of our deepest happiness or darkest depression, our creativity or self-destruction, our problem-solving or problem-making. In its most toxic form it has the potential to be the most potent weapon of mass destruction in the world. In its most cultivated form, it can be a resource for our deepest happiness, and for the flourishing of all humanity – and the planet.

Knowing that so much potential is locked in your mind, why wouldn't you take the time to train and nurture it?

How to use this book

This book invites you on a one-month journey, exploring ancient practices that are now scientifically proven to transform your mind and body for the better. It aims to demystify meditation and to teach you how to train your mind and heart towards greater happiness and wellbeing in your daily life. Consider the next month as an experiment in which you commit to these daily practices, and at the end of the month reflect on the impact it has had on your life.

Each week we'll be covering a specific theme, and you'll find links to unique guided meditations that relate directly to this focus, and which I encourage you to practise on the allocated days. Although doing the same guided meditation for several days in a row may initially seem a bit repetitive, it's only through repetition that the brain can learn new ways of operating, and over time carve out new neural pathways. You'll also find a written version of the guided meditation at the start of each week. This is offered for those who would prefer to read the guidance and then do the practice by themselves in silence.

The purpose of training in mindfulness meditation isn't to become 'better' at meditating, but rather to become 'better' at life. So, along with the daily meditation of the week, the book includes mindful practices to try out each day, which will help you integrate mindfulness into all aspects of your life. Over time and with repetition, these daily practices will become habitual, and you'll start to sense how being mindful can become your default setting, supporting awareness through all aspects of your life.

In Week One we practise bringing our attention to the body and to our senses through the guided body scan and sound meditation, which is the first step to becoming more mindful. We will also integrate mindfulness into daily activities by exploring how you can step into your senses, staying more embodied and present in daily life.

Week Two introduces a breath meditation to help us develop focus. You'll discover daily practices that you can also bring to your work context in order to increase your effectiveness and productivity.

In Week Three we turn our attention inwards, exploring the landscape of thoughts and emotions. We will bring mindfulness to our relationships and discover how this practice can create greater connection to the people in our lives and to the world at large.

Finally, in Week Four we learn the lovingkindness meditation, which helps build connection and compassion in our lives. Then we finish the month with a guided happiness meditation that helps you develop a vision for your greatest happiness.

You'll find guided meditations to use for each week of the program at **www.mindlifeproject.com/book**. Once you have registered your name and email, you will also receive occasional emails with additional mindfulness content to explore. In order to experience the benefits you'll hear about throughout this book, it's important that you commit to this practice. Even on the days when you really don't feel like meditating, have a go anyway. Remember, meditation isn't always going to feel good – in fact, on some days it will really highlight the underlying restlessness or agitation that you may not have noticed because you were too focused on the outside world.

Throughout the book you'll also find recipes that will support you in bringing mindfulness to eating. I've gathered my favourite recipes from dear friends and leading Australian foodie-wellbeing experts, who share recipes that will nourish your body, mind and soul. You'll learn how mindful eating can make you more appreciative of food, and also build awareness around what you choose to eat.

My hope is that as you commit to the practice, you'll start to discover the benefits of a mind that is clear, focused and more present in everyday life.

Through regular practice we start to notice more detail and become more engaged in our whole lives: the exciting parts, the mundane parts and even the difficult parts that we may have previously attempted to avoid. This is where the magic of mindfulness begins.

Before we begin

Firstly, let's talk about the meditation posture

Although we often see pictures of people meditating in a cross-legged lotus position on the floor, you don't have to sit like this to meditate. In fact, I'd encourage you to sit in a chair, or even try lying down, allowing your body to be as comfortable as possible so you can relax and bring all of your energy to training your mind. If you're going to lie down, lie on your back with your legs and arms out straight, palms facing up towards the sky. If you suffer back pain, put a rolled towel or pillow under your knees. Meditation isn't meant to be a physical endurance test, so make sure you're comfortable.

How long should I meditate for?

It's helpful to think about exercise as a metaphor here. If you were training for a marathon, you wouldn't start with a 20-kilometre run. So if you're new to mindfulness, it's best to start with shorter practices and gradually build up over time. I suggest starting with ten minutes a day – the weekly meditations are about this length. The crucial point here is that *some* meditation is better than no meditation. So on those particularly hectic days when you feel like there's not a moment to spare, try to fit in a five-minute practice to keep the habit alive. If you feel inclined you can also do these guided meditations twice a day.

When is the best time to meditate?

There's no right or wrong time to practise, but until you consolidate your meditation into a habit, it's best to choose roughly the same time each day to do it. Depending on your life and your commitments, there will be different times that work best. Consider what time of the day feels easiest for you to stick with and start there. If you choose to meditate at the end of the day and you discover your mind is wild and chaotic, that's not a problem. Just remember the purpose of mindfulness is to become more aware of your state of mind, rather than create a particular state of mind.

What if I can't empty my mind?

This is one of the most common meditation myths brought up in my programs, and it's the reason people quit before they've given it a proper try. Anyone who tries to empty their mind or actively stop their thoughts during meditation will quickly discover that it's basically impossible – in fact, trying to stop your thoughts only makes them more persistent.

The good news is that this is not what we're trying to do. Mindfulness meditation is really about becoming more aware of your mind, observing your thoughts and getting better at letting them go, rather than a complete emptying of the mind.

How do I know if the meditation training is actually working?

As mentioned, the purpose of meditation is not simply to feel calmer while you're meditating. The point of the training is to develop awareness and presence, as this impacts on all areas of your life. As the month progresses, if you commit to the daily meditation practice, you may notice that you …

- Get less stressed by situations that may have previously caused you greater stress.
- Feel more focused at work.
- Are more present in your communication with family and friends.
- Sleep better.
- Worry less.
- Are more aware of your body and its signals.
- Are more aware of your feelings.
- Have the ability to pause before reacting.
- Feel a sense of being part of something bigger than yourself.

TAKE A MOMENT TO CONNECT
WITH YOUR INTENTIONS

When creating any new habit in your life, intention is key.
Take a few moments to think about the following questions
and write down your answers.

What has drawn you to meditation?

What is it that you hope to learn, and how do you hope it
will affect your life?

What might get in the way of you doing your meditation
in the next month and what steps can you take to prioritise
this practice?

Take a few moments to reflect and write down answers to
these questions before you start.

WEEK ONE

Relax the body

Be mindful in everyday life

'The body is your only home in the universe. It is your house of belonging here in the world. It is a very sacred temple. To spend time in silence before the mystery of your body brings you toward wisdom.'
John O'Donohue

Studying medicine expanded my awareness of the exquisite complexity and miracle of the human body. We are born into a body, yet most of us spend our lives not knowing much about its intricacies. We are fascinated by the latest iPhone and quickly learn how to use its new features, but few of us ever learn about the way our eyes help transform light particles and waves into meaningful images in the brain, or how the ears translate wave patterns into the magnificence of a symphony. The more sophisticated a technology, the more invisible it becomes, and the inner workings of the body are a stunning example of this. It's often only when something happens to disrupt one of our senses that we become more conscious of them, and of the complex process that allows us to experience the world.

Our senses are our doorway into the world as we perceive it. They guide us, inform us and enrich our lives. When we wake up in the morning we hear the birds, we see the light and we immediately know it's morning. We feel the cold air and sense our bodies in space, knowing how to get from the bed to the wardrobe to put on warm clothes without needing to consciously think about how to do this. These are simple things we usually don't even notice. However, our bodies are constantly collecting data from the outside world to inform us and drive our behaviours and decisions.

Bringing a more mindful attention to our five physical senses enriches our lives, helping us become more present and embodied. Rather than constantly being lost in our inner world of thoughts, which can pull us out of experience and catapult us into past or future thinking, our senses keep us grounded to what is actually happening from moment to moment.

In a society where many of us are becoming increasingly sedentary and disconnected from our bodies and the environment, it's easy to think that our brains and thoughts are the sole location of our intelligence. But intelligence is distributed throughout the body, and we can enhance this by consciously bringing attention to our physical selves and tuning in to the data that is being captured in every moment. In this way we can harness our entire intelligence to make better decisions and experience life in a richer, more full-bodied way.

During my medical training, learning about the behind-the-scene complexity of our senses brought me into a more embodied experience of being human. Learning about the intricacies of the eye and the physiology of vision brought my attention to the miraculous technology of sight. I learned about the retina, the thin layer of tissue that lines the back of the eye and translates light into electrical nerve signals. This small area of the body contains about 120 million rods, the light receptors that allow us to see in the dark, and 6 million cones, which require more light and are designed to help us perceive colour. This explained why I couldn't see colours in the dark. Prior to studying the body, I'd taken all of my senses for granted, but as I learned about the inner technology of seeing, hearing, tasting and touch, I became more connected to the complete miracle of what previously felt quite ordinary.

There have been many situations where I've found the capacity to stay with my senses particularly valuable. Throughout my career I've given many public talks, and initially I used to get quite nervous. My mind would fill with anxious thoughts that would amplify my fear: 'What if the audience is bored?' or 'What if I don't remember what comes next?' Through practising mindfulness of the senses – feeling my feet on the ground, sensing the movement of my breath, tuning in to the sounds around me – I could shift my attention away from thinking and come back to my body and to the reality of the present moment. In this way, rather than my thoughts amplifying my stress and making my mind foggy and distracted, I could stay embodied and speak from a place of calm presence.

Another situation where this embodied presence has been particularly valuable in my own life is in the context of relationships and communication. When we communicate with others there is a constant stream of data, and we need to make sense of it in order to relate and respond to others. Through developing our ability to tune in to our senses we can more effectively interpret the real meaning of someone's words, and stay connected to what we feel from moment to moment, giving us a better ability to respond. We can also do this while maintaining awareness of the other person's emotional state. This enables more effective communication, and is the basis upon which we can build emotional intelligence, the foundation of wisdom and happiness in our lives.

Bringing mindfulness, this present-moment awareness, to the body and the senses, allows us to stay calm and grounded when the mind is spinning out of control. However, this capacity is a skill, and just like any skill it takes practice to experience its benefits. Just as you wouldn't show up to a marathon without any training, if you want to experience calm and wellbeing in your life, you need to train in the skill of mindfulness when you're not under pressure.

Unlike the mind, which can kidnap our attention and take our thoughts time travelling, the body is a reliable anchor to the present moment.

So in our first week together, we begin by exploring mindfulness of the body and the five physical senses. In the first half of the week you'll be working with the body scan meditation. This meditation will support you in becoming more aware of body sensations, both internally and externally. You're invited to do this meditation every day. Then on day four of this week you'll be introduced to the mindfulness of sound meditation, a chance to practise bringing awareness to the sense of hearing. Along with these formal meditation practices, you'll find daily exercises that will help you integrate mindfulness into your everyday life. As you become more connected to your body, you'll start to become better at recognising and regulating different emotions and stress as they manifest physically.

What do you need to change?

Many of us come to meditation because we're stressed and looking for ways to manage our lives with greater ease. As you will discover in Week Two (page 79), meditation is a powerful practice that helps us shift from stress to calm. However, as you embark on this first week, it's important to be aware of your stress levels, and to consider anything that might prevent you from reaping all the benefits of this new practice.

As you find ways to incorporate the body scan and mindful moments into your day, pay attention to the decisions you are making and how they are adding to your daily stress. See if you can make any small adjustments that could reduce everyday pressure, perhaps by letting go of an expectation or by calling in some extra support. Sometimes simply taking a conscious pause to consider these issues can help you see more clearly and recognise ways to make your life less stressful.

I learned how important this is while in the midst of running the third global Mindful in May campaign. The campaign had gained huge momentum, and as a doctor-turned-social-entrepreneur with no business experience, I was on a steep learning curve. I was incredibly passionate about the impact it was having and had left my secure career in psychiatry to keep the project running.

Although the campaign had by that stage successfully raised sufficient funds to transform the lives of more than ten thousand people by building clean water wells in developing countries, I was still working hard to make it financially viable and provide a wage for myself and a team. My eighty-hour work weeks were exhilarating, but my determination was pushing me beyond my physical limits. It was only when the campaign ended that I hit burnout. Suddenly – and seemingly out of nowhere – I experienced intense anxiety. There was a continuous tightness in my lungs and throat, and I had fearful thoughts about what the physical symptoms might mean. Although on one level, through mindfulness, I was able to recognise my fears as irrational, they were nevertheless highly uncomfortable and unpleasant. I recognised this as an amygdala on overdrive and upped my dose of meditation, basically enrolling myself in a home-based intensive solo meditation retreat to help calm my nervous system and regain an inner balance.

Things settled over time, but the irony wasn't lost on me: through running a meditation campaign, I'd burned myself out. Apart from my body being completely run down, I felt that I'd somehow failed to walk my talk.

The reality was that despite the fact that I was meditating, the stress and demand of running a start-up outweighed the capacity of a meditation practice to keep my nervous system balanced. It reminded me of patients I'd treated, people with diabetes who believed that their medication allowed them to increase the amount of chocolate and ice-cream they ate, as though the food was somehow being buffered by the effect of their tablets.

I shared this experience with the Mindful in May community and recognised that this was an opportunity to activate self-compassion, a key ingredient of mindfulness training, rather than fall into self-criticism. Through the lens of compassion I could acknowledge that I was doing the best I could while on a very steep learning curve. I took some time to reflect on how to move forward, and I realised that I needed to take more financial risk in order to get support in running the campaign. The following year, I was able to grow the campaign, learn from my mistakes and maintain my health in the process.

It was a potent reminder that we can't just tack meditation onto our hectic lives and expect complete protection from the very real impacts of chronic stress. Rather, it's a wellbeing practice that is a powerful complement to, but not a replacement for, structuring our lives in alignment with good health practices and meaningful values.

So this week, as you start to connect with the body and the senses, take time to reflect on your life and work, and see if there are any adjustments you can make to ease the pressure and find more balance.

Day One

THE BODY SCAN

'You must learn to be still in the midst of activity,
and to be vibrantly alive in repose.'
Indira Gandhi

When I first started learning mindfulness I was very confused by the body scan – I wondered how this practice could possibly help me. One of the biggest challenges for me was dealing with the boredom and restlessness. As a driven and ambitious person, I found that lying down and doing the body scan felt like a waste of time. However, knowing the neuroscience of mindfulness really helped me stick with it despite the difficulties, because I knew that if I kept doing it, I was literally going to change my brain circuits for the better.

The guided body scan meditation (which you'll find online at **www.mindlifeproject.com/book**) brings our attention to the present moment by tuning in to sensations in the body. Often if we've been very active and busy, lying down can quickly lead to sleep. In this practice, the aim is to stay awake, teaching the body and mind how to be alert and relaxed at the same time. If you do feel drowsy, try the meditation with your eyes open, or take a few deep breaths to energise yourself.

It takes a while to feel the benefits of the practice, and on some days you're going to face thoughts that seem like major obstacles. We've all had them, the ones that tell you, 'I'm too tired for this today,' or, 'I don't think this is really helping me,' or, 'I'll just do it tomorrow,' or, 'I've got some work I really need to get done.' Be aware of these sabotaging thoughts, and do the practice in spite of them.

One strategy I've found that's been particularly helpful on days like these is to sit for just one minute of practice. When I do this I often end up completing a full practice, because committing to that first, manageable step helps me overcome the initial resistance.

So this week try to do the body scan *every day*. You can keep track of your observations and questions in *The Happiness Plan* meditation journal, which you can download from the resource page **www.mindlifeproject.com/book**.

BE KIND TO THE PUPPY

Training the mind takes enormous patience. If you're just beginning, you'll quickly discover how frustrating it can be to keep your mind focused. A famous ancient meditation metaphor likens training the mind to training a puppy. When you sit to meditate, imagine your mind is an innocent, untrained puppy, full of energy and bouncing around all over the place. Just as you would bring a kind, patient attitude to teaching your puppy how to 'stay', make sure you notice the attitude you are bringing to your meditation practice. Be sure to be kind and gentle when you discover your mind doesn't want to 'stay'.

BODY SCAN GUIDANCE

Purpose

- To develop more stable attention and focus, becoming aware of the mind's tendency to wander.
- To become more tuned into the body on a daily basis and become better at noticing when the body is holding tension.
- To develop the capacity to observe experience without reacting to it – the first step to reducing emotional reactivity and increasing emotional intelligence.

The practice

- Before you switch on the guided body scan, make sure you find a comfortable and quiet place where you won't be disturbed.
- It is preferable to do the practice lying down. If you have back pain, place a rolled-up towel or pillow under your knees.

Tips

- If you feel yourself falling asleep, try keeping your eyes open, or take some deep breaths to energise yourself.
- Bring the curiosity of a scientist to the body scan, noticing whatever arises, including thoughts, feelings and sensations, and allowing them to come and go.
- If difficult feelings like boredom, restlessness, judgement or impatience arise, just allow them to become part of the practice, noticing whatever is present in each

moment, whether pleasant, unpleasant or neutral and bring a kind, compassionate attitude to yourself.

You can listen to the body scan meditation by visiting www.mindlifeproject.com/book

A condensed transcript of the practice is included below in case you'd prefer to read it and guide yourself through.

Body scan meditation guidance

1. Make yourself as comfortable as possible, lying on the floor with your head supported, arms by your side, palms facing up, legs straight out in front of you and allowing your feet to comfortably fall to the sides.

2. Gently close your eyes.

3. Let go of any concerns about the past or future for this short time.

4. Becoming aware of the body lying there, notice any areas of contact between the body and the floor.

5. Take a deep breath in and gently let it go.

6. Now, allow the breath to find its natural rhythm.

7. Become aware of any sensations connected to the breath as it flows in and out of the body.

8. Notice any areas of tension in the body, and with each outbreath release any tightness, allowing the body to soften as if melting into the floor.

9. Notice any sensations in the body: sense temperature, movement of air across the skin, tingling or perhaps no sensations at all.

10. Now, gently bring your attention to the feet; feel the pressure of both heels resting on the floor, rest your attention on the toes, the spaces between the toes, and notice any sensations present in the feet.

11. Move your attention through the body, part by part, working up the legs to the chest, from the palms up to the shoulders and on up to your forehead. And if thoughts or feelings arise, just notice them, let them go and direct your attention back to sensations in the body.

12. Allow your awareness now to expand and include a sense of the whole body lying in stillness.

13. Take a few moments at the end of this practice to bring gratitude to the many parts of the body that function miraculously from moment to moment, whether with or without your attention.

14. When you are ready, gently wriggle your fingers and toes and remember you can check in to the sensations of the body as a way of tuning in to yourself and becoming more mindful and present at any moment of the day.

Practise the guided body scan for the first three days of this week, and complete the daily mindful exercises that follow.

DON'T WORRY ABOUT THE WATERFALL

During meditation it's not uncommon to be overwhelmed by the constant flood of thoughts. Often this experience has been described as the 'waterfall' of the mind. So know that you are not alone, and that this is not something particular to your mind; it's the nature of all minds. Mindfulness doesn't stop you from thinking, but it helps you recognise the movement of the mind without getting carried away by it.

Many people come to meditation hoping to switch off or calm down, and so discovering this waterfall can be unsettling. You may feel meditation is making you feel worse or more agitated. However, recognising this constant inner chatter is the first step to working with your mind more effectively.

Aside from the formal guided body scan meditation that you're invited to use each day this week, you can develop greater presence in daily life through 'incidental' mindfulness practices. These will amplify the effects of your mindfulness meditation training, and support you in reconnecting with your body and coming back to the present moment. Like any new skill, as you repeat these practices over and over, they will become automatic. You'll begin to naturally return to the present moment and get less carried away by your thoughts.

Throughout the week we will be exploring many incidental mindfulness practices, but today we start with the 'mindful STOP'.

TODAY'S PRACTICE
The Mindful STOP

This practice is a way of pausing and physically catching your breath throughout the day. It's a quick and simple way to remember to connect with yourself, which creates greater potential for presence and wisdom in daily life.

Steps to practising the mindful STOP

S – Stop.

T – Take three mindful breaths, feeling the sensation of the breath flowing.

O – Observe the body, notice any tension and actively let it go.

P – Proceed with your day.

Set an alarm on your phone to ring at four random times during the day with the word STOP. You could also write the word STOP on some sticky notes and leave them in places you regularly see, such as the shower, the toilet, on your laptop, or in your car. When you see these reminders, pause for a few moments to practise the STOP exercise. As you continue to practice the guided body scan each day and the STOP practice this week, remember that …

… the purpose of mindfulness is not to create a particular state of mind, but rather to be aware of whatever state is present.

Just like getting physically fit, you need to commit to the practice to experience the results of a mind that is functioning at its best.

Day Two

COME BACK TO THE BODY

'Let tiny drops of stillness fall gently through my day.'
Noel Davis

How did your first body scan go?

When I first began meditating it took time for me to feel comfortable tuning in to the sensations in my body. In fact it wasn't until I discovered some fascinating neuroscience about a few crucial brain circuits, that the purpose of the body scan and this practice of tuning in to the senses started to 'make sense'.

To explore these brain circuits and their impact, imagine for a moment that you're out for dinner with a friend at one of your favourite restaurants. You're really excited to see them, but you've got a stressful work presentation the next day. Rather than actually enjoying the meal and being present with your friend, you get lost in thoughts about whether you're prepared enough, and you can't stop thinking of things you need to do. Rather than enjoying the actual experience of tasting the meal, you're caught up in worry and anxiety.

The research describes two different brain circuits that lead to different ways of experiencing our lives, each determined by where we are focusing our attention. If we understand these circuits we can learn how to use them to our advantage.

The first brain circuit is called the 'default mode network', and is associated with thoughts about ourselves – the story of 'me'. The default circuit often gets us lost in thoughts about the future, worrying about how we're going to get things done, and analysing and judging ourselves along the way. It is activated when we are in daydream mode and not focused on anything in particular.

The second brain circuit is called the 'direct experience network', and this one is active when we are doing something focused and goal-driven. It's the brain circuit that is activated when you are experiencing reality directly through your body and senses. This 'direct experience' circuit lets you taste the flavours of the meal you're eating and taste your wine without thinking about what you need to do tomorrow. Rather than narrating, analysing and evaluating the experience, by coming back to the body you are shifting your attention away from thoughts and back to a direct experience of your reality.

Scientists have discovered that these two circuits operate like an accelerator and brake on a car: they can't be activated at the same time.

Both the 'default mode' and 'direct experience' circuits play a role in helping us make sense of our lives. We need the direct circuit to help us absorb the world around us, but we need the default circuit to help us create a sense of our identity and life story. However, research has shown that too much activity in the default circuit is associated with excessive self-absorbed thinking, depression and anxiety.

Mindfulness strengthens our capacity to know which brain circuit is active from moment to moment, and to become better at consciously switching from one to the other. Through regular mindfulness practice we strengthen the 'direct' experience circuits and improve our ability to get out of our heads and into our bodies – a valuable skill, especially when our thoughts are adding to our stress.

TODAY'S PRACTICE
The Mindful Shower

Make sure you do the body scan meditation again today. Although you will be using the same guidance (which you can find here **www.mindlifeproject.com/book**), each time you meditate you may notice that the experience is quite different.

As well as completing the guided meditation, activate the direct experience circuits by bringing mindfulness to your shower. Rather than being lost in thought during your shower, direct your attention to your senses as a way of anchoring yourself to the present moment.

The four steps to having a mindful shower

1. Once you're in the shower and the water is on, bring your attention to the sensations of water touching your skin.
2. Feel the temperature.
3. Tune in to sounds and listen to the water.
4. When you notice the mind has become lost in thinking and you've lost touch with the feeling of water on your body, gently bring your attention back to the body and sense the water on your skin.

Bring mindfulness of the body to other ordinary moments in your day

A mindful tea break

- Tune in to your sense of sight and notice the colour of the tea.
- Tune in to the smell of the tea.
- Tune in to your sense of touch and feel the warmth of the cup on your skin and the temperature of the tea in your mouth.
- Tune in to taste as you sip your tea and notice the different flavours and where in your mouth you sense taste.

Doing the dishes mindfully

- Tune in to sight and notice the dirty plates.
- Tune in to the sound of water flowing from the tap.
- Tune in to touch as you feel the water on your hands and sense the movement of your hands as you wash the dishes.
- When you notice your mind wandering into thinking, activate your direct experience circuits by coming back to your senses.

Mindful driving

- Tune in to the touch and feel of your hands on the steering wheel and your body in the seat. Notice your posture and release any tension in the body as you drive.
- Tune in to the sight of cars around you, notice the colour of the car in front of you.
- Tune in to sound and experiment with turning the radio off and simply driving in silence.

Day Three

MINDFUL EATING

*'The world is full of magic things, patiently waiting
for our senses to grow sharper.'*
WB Yeats

Did you find time to practise the body scan yesterday?

How was your mindful shower?

When I was introduced to the mindful shower practice, I remember feeling some resistance, because I considered my shower an opportunity to think and organise myself. But these incidental mindfulness practices are not a waste of time. They're highly efficient ways to strengthen new mental habits, specifically the habit of being more present in daily life. Once you've consolidated this habit, you'll have a better capacity to *choose* how you want to use your mind, rather than have it run the show.

As you train yourself to stay present to your senses, it will likely highlight how your mind habitually disconnects and gets lost in thinking. As you'll discover, although thinking is a powerful tool that can offer us original, creative ideas and solutions to problems, a lot of the time our thoughts are repetitive, uncreative, and frequently just add to our stress.

Today, as a way of continuing to return to your senses, I suggest that you try out mindful eating. Many of us tend to eat in a rush, or while focused on other things – often we don't even taste our food, and so we end up eating more than we need. Because of this, mindful eating has recently become a popular weight loss practice: rather than the severe restraints of traditional dieting, mindful eating makes you more aware of what you are putting in your mouth and when you feel full.

This exercise will not only continue to build neural pathways that support focused attention and presence, but it will also make eating more enjoyable. As someone with a sweet tooth, I've found it helps me savour sweets more slowly and leaves me feeling more satisfied with one piece of chocolate, rather than eating an entire block!

TODAY'S PRACTICE
Mindful Eating

You can do this with any piece of food, but try it with a piece of chocolate, preferably dark chocolate, as it's healthier than milk chocolate and has more depth of flavour (some people prefer to use a sultana).

1. Put the piece of chocolate in your palm and imagine you have never eaten this food before.
2. Move through each of your senses, tuning in completely to all the information you can take in through each sense.
   - **Sight:** notice all the colours, shapes, shadows and light.
   - **Touch:** holding the chocolate in your hand, notice its weight, firmness, edges, dryness or moisture.

- **Taste:** place the chocolate in your mouth and don't chew. Instead, move it around your mouth and sense the flavour. Start eating the chocolate very slowly while staying completely attentive to your sense of taste. Notice where you sense the flavours – is it at the back of the tongue or the front? Notice what side of your mouth you habitually chew on.

3. As you move through the practice, notice any thoughts that arise, and when you notice you've been caught in thinking, just let go of the thoughts and come back to whatever sense you are exploring.

I once witnessed a powerful breakthrough during a guided mindful eating exercise in one of my workshops. In this group we used a sultana instead of chocolate. After the exercise, a participant confessed that she'd had a phobia of sultanas for most of her life, and that she'd initially felt resistant, wanting to leave the workshop. Sharing this she laughed, as did everyone else (admittedly, I hadn't come across many sultana phobias during my career in psychiatry). Despite her fear, she tried it out, knowing she could stop if it got too unpleasant. She was surprised and delighted to discover that the sultana wasn't as bad as she'd anticipated.

The exercise demonstrated to her how she had been caught up in a habitual belief, based on past experience, that was determining her current reality. It made her wonder what other assumptions and fears she might be holding onto as facts – thoughts that were closing off opportunities in other parts of her life.

Mindfulness asks us to step into what's referred to as 'the beginner's mind', a mind that meets experience with openness and curiosity. As we bring this fresh perspective to life, we become more aware of when our automatic responses are being triggered. This awareness gives us an opportunity to live beyond the limitations of our patterned responses.

Day Four

MINDFULNESS OF SOUND MEDITATION

'Listen to silence, it has so much to say.'
Rumi

Today we shift to the guided sound meditation.

Being mindful of sounds is another way of training our attention to be where we want it to be. Through this practice we explore how mindfulness can connect us more deeply to the environment around us and to the people in our lives.

Instead of relating to sounds around us as a distraction from our meditation, for the next few days we actually use sounds as the anchor for our practice. This means that if you're meditating and your neighbour's car alarm goes off, this repetitive beeping just becomes part of the meditation.

When you're meditating and you hear a sound that grabs your attention, see if you can notice your reaction. If the sound happens to be unpleasant and triggers an emotion such as irritation, practise allowing the irritation to be present, simply noticing this feeling rather than trying to change it. In this way mindfulness meditation helps develop our frustration threshold, which in turn helps us find emotional balance. As American novelist and political activist Anne Lamott wisely wrote, 'It's good to do uncomfortable things. It's weight training for life.'

The triggers we discover during our meditation practice often reflect where we get easily triggered in life. If you can relate to feeling like you 'can't stand it' when an unpleasant sound intrudes into your meditation, you could be suffering from what psychologist Albert Ellis called 'can't-stand-it-itis', and no doubt if you reflect on your daily life, you may find that you have a tendency to get easily frustrated when things aren't quite how you want them to be.

Today, replace the body scan with the guided sound meditation every day, until we move to the next meditation in Week Two (you'll find it online at **www.mindlifeproject.com/book**).

MINDFULNESS OF SOUND GUIDANCE

Purpose

- To tune in to the sense of sound and train the mind to focus attention on sounds that arise in the external world without getting caught up in them.
- To develop a more stable attention and focus, becoming aware of the mind's tendency to wander.

The practice

- This practice can be done in any environment. Unlike other practices, which are most easily done in a relatively quiet space where you won't be disturbed, sounds are now the focus of your attention.

Tips

- Once you've done this practice for a few days with guidance, try it out on your own as you move through your day. Use the changing sounds around you as a way of coming back to the present moment.
- As a way of engaging your attention, notice the sounds you can hear from closest to furthest.
- Notice that you may have a preference for some sounds over others, but see if you can just allow sounds to be as they are without pushing the unpleasant ones away. In this way, you'll be learning how to stay with unpleasant experiences, which builds resilience.

You can listen to this guided meditation by visiting www.mindlifeproject.com/book

Mindfulness of sound meditation guidance

As with all mindfulness meditation, it is important to ensure the body is relaxed and comfortable. This practice is preferably done in a seated position (but you can lie down if you prefer).

1. We start the practice by tuning in to the rhythm of the breath.
2. Then simply shift attention to the sounds that come and go, each moment, wherever you are.
3. If there are no sounds then just notice the silence.
4. Notice as you pay attention to the sounds whether you are drawn to any in particular, and notice whether some sounds are pleasant, unpleasant or neutral.

Notice the way sounds can so easily stimulate stories that hijack your attention, and remember to turn on your meditation GPS (gentleness, patience and a sense of humour) as you practice.

TODAY'S PRACTICE
Tune in to Sounds in Everyday Life

As a way of bringing the mindfulness of sound practice into your daily life, try this:

1. Choose a place that is full of sounds (i.e. the train on the way to work, your office, a cafe, the supermarket).
2. Decide that you will practice mindfulness of sound for five minutes while you either sit or move through the environment.
3. Set your timer for five minutes.
4. Use sounds in the environment as an anchor for your attention just as you've been using the sensations in your body.
5. Notice sounds as they come and go, and notice any reactions you have to sounds that you may or may not like.
6. Rather than chasing or actively searching for sounds, just keep your awareness and attention on the soundscape and allow sounds to come and go.
7. If you notice your mind has gotten caught up in thinking, simply recognise this, let go of the thoughts and bring your attention back to the sounds.

You can also explore bringing mindfulness to sounds when listening to music or a favourite podcast.

Try out this mindful music exercise

1. Choose a piece of music you love.
2. Set aside some uninterrupted time to practice mindful listening, which will allow you to be fully present to the music.

3. Lie down, turn the music on and use the sounds as the anchor of this meditation.

4. Tune in to the different instruments in the piece, notice the sounds and the space between the sounds, notice how the music makes you feel.

5. When you notice your mind wandering or getting caught up in thinking or to-do lists, recognise this and simply let go of the thoughts, bringing your attention back to the music.

6. Notice how this way of listening to music is different from how you may normally listen.

You can try this practice with live music too, and notice how much richer the experience is when you are fully present in it.

Day Five

MINDFUL WALKING

*'Don't think that only sitting with the eyes closed is meditation practice.
Steady practice is keeping mindful in every posture, whether sitting,
walking, standing or lying down.'*
Ajahn Chah

Did you make the time to do the new guided sound meditation?

Keep practising the meditation each day this week and don't forget you can tune in to the sounds around you as a way of getting out of your head and into your body, connecting with the present moment.

So far we've explored daily mindful practices that focus on bringing your attention to the different senses. Today's practice, mindful walking, offers you a way to strengthen your mindful muscle while tuning in to all five of your senses as you simply walk.

Over recent years, I've been inspired by watching my mother walk her very frail elderly dog every day. Rather than get impatient at the extremely slow pace of her companion, my mother has turned it into an opportunity for mindful walking. What could have become a burden has now become a daily wake-up call and reminder to slow down and be fully present. Likewise, as a parent, it's easy to get impatient walking with very young children. However, this too is an opportunity to slow down and step into our lives with more presence.

Mindful walking is a way to put mindfulness into motion, and it's easy to integrate it into your life. Whether it's a leisurely walk on the beach or briskly moving between places, the essence of the practice is to bring your attention to all of the sensations of walking, rather than getting lost in your thoughts. Mindful walking helps you unhook from compulsive thinking, making to-do lists or analysing problems, and brings you back to an awareness of your body. In *Dubliners*, writer James Joyce beautifully captures *unmindful* walking in a brief description of one his characters: 'Mr Duffy lived a short distance from his body.' So many of us are completely cut off from our physical selves, as if the body was designed purely to transport our overactive brains from one place to another. Mindful walking reminds us to bring awareness to our whole being, almost like a body scan in motion.

This is a practice that you can do for any length of time in any situation where you find yourself moving from one point to another, whether it's a day-long hike in a national park or a five-minute walk down the street.

TODAY'S PRACTICE
Mindful Walking

1. **Set an intention to start mindful walking.** Be clear in your own mind that you are going to stay present to the feeling of walking rather than getting lost in your thoughts. The aim is to notice when

you mentally detach from your body, walking on automatic pilot as you move from A to B. Try to move with an ongoing awareness of walking itself.

2. **Set a time or a distance for your mindful walk.** You might like to make a habit of walking mindfully every time you are in a particular setting. If you're at work you might designate a particular corridor as your mindful walking reminder. Each time you pass through that corridor, intentionally direct your attention to the body, giving your mind a micro-break. If you regularly walk on the beach, in a park or in the street, you might choose a stretch of path between two landmarks as your mindful walking distance.

3. **Bring your attention into your body and out of your head.** Sense your feet on the ground, slow your walking down slightly and notice the lifting and placing of your feet on the ground. You may like to silently note 'lift' and 'place'. Sense your legs and notice the sensation of balancing. Tune in to your senses and notice the sounds around you, including smells, colours, light and shadows.

TIP FOR WALKING

If you notice yourself walking in a hurry during the day, recognise the feeling of rushing in your body and take a moment to stop. Take three mindful breaths, bring your awareness into your body, and take a few slow footsteps to break the rush and come back to presence.

This is an opportunity to get out of the whirlwind of your thoughts, even if just for a few minutes.

Day Six

MINDFUL SEEING

*'When the eyes and ears are open, even the leaves on
the trees teach like pages from the scriptures.'*
Kabir

How was the experience of mindful walking?

What did you discover?

What about the sound meditation? Did you find that challenging?

As you become more familiar with the sound meditation, you may like to explore doing it without guidance. Start by setting up a timer, and be your own guide. Begin with a short practice of two minutes and simply tune in to the sounds around you, and each time your attention wanders, bring it back to sounds.

I've often wondered what life would be like if I couldn't hear, see, taste, smell or feel. A number of years ago this curiosity led me to New York, where I made a short documentary exploring what it would be like to be blind in one of the busiest cities in the world. There I met

Frank Senior, a blind jazz musician from the Bronx who I followed over several months. We first met on Fifth Avenue in the Upper East Side, at his newsstand. I was nervous and awkward; I'd never interacted with someone who was blind before. Luckily, Frank was a friendly, open guy who loved bringing people into his world. As we walked arm in arm down Fifth Avenue he laughed, saying, 'Girl, you're holding on real tight, it's okay, you can relax.'

I noticed how comfortable I felt talking to Frank, as if his blindness somehow offered a safe space for my own self-disclosure.

'When sighted people are around blind people,' Frank explained, 'because they know we can't see, they kind of let their hair down, they open it up, they expose themselves. I don't do anything but be blind.'

Through my time with Frank, I became acutely aware of the gift of my own eyes, but also of the many incorrect assumptions I had held about how being blind would limit someone in their life.

'People think being blind is not being aware,' Frank reflected. 'They know deep down inside that's not so, it's just that when they close their eyes, they're lost.'

So many of us see the world, but remain blind to the miracles around us.

In her famous essay 'Three Days to See', Helen Keller, one of the 20th century's leading humanitarians, who was blind and deaf, provided a perfect invitation for practising mindful seeing. Keller described asking a friend what she'd seen during a walk in the woods, and the friend replied, 'Nothing in particular.' Keller was astounded at the thought.

How was it possible, I asked myself, to walk for an hour through the woods and see nothing worthy of note? I who cannot see find hundreds of things to interest me through mere touch. I feel the delicate symmetry of a leaf. I pass my hands lovingly about the smooth skin of a silver birch, or the rough, shaggy bark of a pine. In Spring I touch the branches of trees hopefully in search of a bud, the first sign of awakening nature after her winter's sleep … To me the pageant of seasons is a thrilling and unending drama, the action of which streams through my fingertips. At times my heart cries out with longing to see all these things.

If I can get so much pleasure from mere touch, how much more beauty must be revealed by sight.

TODAY'S PRACTICE
Mindful Seeing

Imagine today is the last day you will ever see. How would this change the way you pay attention?

Could you hold the image of those you love in your mind's eye?

Today, as you move through the day, notice all of the aspects of sight. Notice your ability to see colour, shapes, distance, and movement. Take a walk to your local park and become interested in this phenomenon of seeing with appreciation and curiosity. Notice how bringing presence to our ordinary moments can spark gratitude and wonder, where before there may have been monotony and indifference.

Day Seven

MAKE MEDITATION A HABIT

*'This very moment, we can change our lives. There never was a moment,
and never will be, when we are without the power to alter our destiny.
This second, we can turn the tables on resistance.'*
Steven Pressfield

As you move through the first week of daily meditation practice, the
novelty may start to wear off. You may fall victim to the many excuses
that emerge in your mind, convincing you not to meditate. As with any
new behaviour that we want to build into our routine, developing a
regular meditation practice can be really challenging.

We've all experienced this kind of resistance to a new practice,
whether we're attempting to meditate regularly, eat well, or start a
new exercise routine. Through understanding how to create habits, you
can overcome this inner resistance and make mindfulness a regular
part of your life.

When I started meditating many years ago, I found it hard to make it a habit. Somehow it was easy to let it be nudged off the to-do list by seemingly more urgent and important things. My lack of understanding around the science of habit formation, combined with some aspects of my thinking, kept me from making progress.

Here were a few of the obstacles that were in my way. Can you relate to any of them?

- **All-or-nothing thinking:** this style of thinking makes you believe that if you are not doing something one hundred per cent correctly, you may as well not be doing it at all. This can really inhibit your ability to keep any habit alive.

- **Setting unrealistic goals:** many meditation courses require you to meditate for thirty or forty minutes a day. When we're starting out with any new behaviour, it's often better to start off small until we've made it part of our routine, and then gradually build up towards longer periods of practice. Setting unrealistic goals will inevitably sabotage your attempts to form a regular habit.

It wasn't until I came upon the powerful teaching of BJ Fogg, a Stanford professor and world expert in habit formation, that I found a way to overcome these obstacles. Fogg gave me three key tips that have been invaluable in supporting my own habit of meditation:

1. **Start with a practice that will take you less than sixty seconds**
    In the case of meditation, if ten minutes every day is proving too much to maintain, try committing to just one minute a day and building it up by a few minutes each week. You can find my mindful

minute meditation at www.mindlifeproject.com/book, which you can use multiple times throughout the day.

2. **Choose a reliable anchor**

   You need to anchor your new behaviour (in this case meditation) to something that is already a habit in your life. For example, you might decide that you're going to do your mindful meditation in the car before you leave for work, or directly after you brush your teeth.

3. **Give yourself active recognition and positive reinforcement**

   Once you've done your daily meditation practice, make sure you give yourself positive reinforcement. BJ Fogg has found that this stimulates the pleasure centres in our brain and increases the likelihood that we'll persist with an activity.

Congratulations on completing

WEEK ONE

You've made it through your first week of mindfulness practice. Chances are that there have been moments during this week when you've struggled to complete your meditation, or found yourself acting mindlessly at exactly the moment when you would have liked to remain present and focused.

If so, don't feel disheartened, because this is a very normal experience. As with any new project, when you begin a meditation practice, it's common to fall short of your expectations. The important thing is not to give up, and to be kind to yourself throughout the process.

Many of us believe that being harsh with ourselves is the best way to be productive and get things done – I know this from personal experience. However, in a conversation I had with world-leading self-compassion researcher Kristin Neff, I learned how this inner critic can harm our health, our relationships and our happiness:

There are a lot of reasons people aren't self-compassionate, but probably the number one reason is that people think they need to be harshly self-critical to motivate themselves. They think that if they're kind and encouraging, they'll basically be lazy and passive and not reach their goals.

In fact, Neff's research shows that people who are encouraging and supportive of themselves are more likely to reach their goals, and what's really significant is that if they fail to reach their goals, they're more likely to try again.

What is self-compassion?

Kristin Neff defines self-compassion as having three components:

1. **An attitude of kindness and care towards yourself**
   Rather than driving yourself with the 'whip of self-criticism', you relate to yourself as you would relate to a good friend: with care, gentleness and support.

2. **A recognition that our shared humanity reduces isolation**
   Loss and disappointment are inevitable parts of life, yet when things don't go our way, it's easy to fall into a victim mentality and wonder, 'Why is this happening to me?' With self-compassion we can use these experiences as opportunities to connect more deeply with others, reminding ourselves that all humans experience loss, disappointment and suffering.

3. **The capacity to turn towards challenges with mindfulness**
   Our natural instinct is to avoid or push away difficult experiences.

Mindfulness is a crucial ingredient of self-compassion, as it allows us to recognise what is happening and acknowledge our emotions. We can bring kindness and gentleness to ourselves when we are suffering, and we are able to move through the emotion. Through mindfulness we process our emotions, rather than getting stuck in them or using avoidance behaviours such as overeating, drinking or workaholism to try and soothe ourselves.

Research has demonstrated that people who have greater self-compassion experience less depression and anxiety, and greater happiness and life satisfaction. Neff further explains:

Self-compassion embraces suffering and wraps it in a sense of loving, connected presence – a positive emotion. So self-compassion alleviates the suffering of the negative mind states at the same time as it generates positive ones. It does this simultaneously, and it does it without the sugar-coating of thinking 'everything's okay'. It says 'No, everything's not okay, the present is not okay, but can I be kind and caring towards myself?'

As you start to pay attention to your own inner dialogue, it can be quite shocking to discover how self-critical you are. If you grew up with very critical parents you probably learned to talk to yourself that way, but it's also a reflection of our own unique temperaments. Through increased self-awareness, cultivated through mindfulness, it's possible to shift the quality of this self-talk and move towards a more loving relationship with ourselves.

Our minds are intimately connected to our bodies, and the kind of thoughts we have impact our physiology. Take a moment to bring to mind something you love: maybe it's an image of a beautiful beach, or someone you care about. You may notice how just thinking about this image calms and relaxes your body, perhaps lowering your heart rate and slowing your breath. Similarly, when you remember something that's upset you in the past, you can feel the impact of that thought on your emotional state and in your body – your stomach churning, or perhaps a tightening in your throat.

When we have self-critical thoughts, we actually trigger areas of the brain that are associated with stress. If we do this over a long time, it leads to high levels of cortisol (the stress hormone) in the body. In contrast to that, self-compassion is associated with a different system, the 'tend-and-befriend' system. When we practice self-compassion, we're caring for ourselves like a mother cares for a distressed baby, activating this tend-and-befriend system and releasing oxytocin (the love molecule), which reduces the level of cortisol in the body.

A SELF–COMPASSION EXERCISE

If you find yourself in a difficult situation where you're angry, disappointed or anxious, or things just haven't gone the way you wanted, take a moment to actually put your hand on your heart as a way of actively caring for yourself (touch is a powerful way to self-soothe and activate the tend-and-befriend system). You can also add soothing words such as, 'This feels really hard', 'I'm not alone – imagine all the humans that are suffering in this moment', 'May I be kind to myself'.

BELLY FOOD

Nurture your insides, your overall
health and your mind

Over the past week you've been developing awareness of your whole body and gradually becoming more attuned to subtle sensations and emotions that you may not previously have been aware of. Through this expanded awareness you are getting deeper access to the intelligence of your whole body.

Recent research has identified the literal 'brain in your gut'. If you've ever felt butterflies in your stomach when you were anxious, or made a decision based on a 'gut feeling', then you've been getting messages from the more than one hundred million nerve cells that line your gastrointestinal tract and control digestion. We now understand that there is in fact a two-way communication between the gut and the brain. In other words, whereas previously scientists believed that our emotions led to problems with digestion, it is now suggested that the reverse is also true.

In his book *Good Gut*, Justin Sonnenburg, Stanford professor of microbiology and immunology, explains the impact of our gut bacteria on our mood:

Not only is our brain 'aware' of our gut microbes, but these bacteria can influence our perception of the world and alter our behaviour. It is becoming clear that the influence of our microbiota reaches far beyond the gut to affect an aspect of our biology few would have predicted: our mind.

The gut bacteria work together to influence the body's levels of the potent neurotransmitter serotonin, which regulates feelings of happiness.

Nurture your gut microbiome, and your physical and mental wellbeing, with these recipes.

Quinoa hotcakes

By Amy Crawford
www.theholisticingredient.com
Serves 1

Quinoa, while used much like a grain, is actually a seed. It is very gentle on your digestive system, and contains B vitamins and fibre that nourish your digestive tract. Delicious, light hotcakes are a great way to start your day.

½ cup cooked quinoa

1 egg

1 tbsp quinoa flour, or flour of choice

2 tsp rice malt syrup (or sweetener of choice, to taste)

2 tsp lemon juice

1 heaped tsp grated lemon rind

A good pinch of vanilla powder (or essence)

Pinch of salt

2 tsp coconut oil (for the pan)

In a small bowl, combine all above ingredients except coconut oil. Put your frying pan on the stove on medium heat. When hot, add your coconut oil. Spoon in your hot cakes (it should make 2–3). Cook for 3–4 minutes on one side or until golden. Using a spatula, very carefully turn them over (they are quite delicate).

Top with your choice of topping: Greek yoghurt drizzled with leftover syrup and lemon rind is one simple option.

Thai veg with cashew & tempeh

By Sun Hyland

www.newearthcatering.com

Serves 2–3

Fermented foods such as **tempeh** and **miso** are filled with healthy live micro-organisms that crowd out the bad gut bacteria. This allows for better absorption of minerals and enhances overall wellbeing.

200g plain tempeh

1 green capsicum

1 bunch spring onion

1 head broccoli

1 large zucchini

1 bunch bok choy

50g ginger

1 tin coconut cream

3 kaffir lime leaves

1½ tsp salt

1½ tsp coconut or palm sugar

60g coconut butter

30ml tamari

¼ cup water

Heat your pan. (A wok is best, otherwise use a large, heavy-based pan. In either case ensure you have a lid that fits.) Slice the tempeh into 6–8mm even slices. Melt half the coconut butter in the pan and carefully add the slices of tempeh. Cook at medium heat until lightly browned on both sides. Turn off the heat and pour the tamari over the tempeh while it's still hot. When cool enough, slice into 2cm pieces.

Clean the spring onions, discarding any floppy green parts. Chop the white parts into 1cm slices. Put the green parts aside. Finely dice the ginger. Chop the capsicum into 1cm chunks, slice the broccoli and zucchini into bite-sized pieces, and roughly chop bok choy.

Heat the remaining coconut butter in the wok. Add the ginger, capsicum and spring onion. Fry gently until soft. Add the broccoli and zucchini and fry for a couple of minutes. Turn the flame up fairly high. Add the water, put the lid on quickly. Steam the veg in the pan like this for 3 minutes.

Turn the heat down. Remove the lid and add the coconut cream, salt, sugar and kaffir lime leaves. Simmer gently for about five minutes.

Add the tempeh and bok choy, mix through and cook for a further minute with the lid on – just enough to heat the tempeh through.

Serve on jasmine rice with fresh chilli and crushed peanuts. Slice the green parts of the spring onions thinly to use as a garnish.

Crispy tofu & broccolini salad

Sun Hyland

www.newearthcatering.com

Serves 3

Broccolini and other cruciferous vegetables including kale, cabbage and cauliflower, contain glucosinolates. When broken down by the gut, glucosinolates release anti-inflammatory substances that reduce the risk of bladder, breast, colon, liver, lung and stomach cancer. Studies have demonstrated that people who eat the most cruciferous vegetables have an eighteen per cent reduced risk of colorectal cancer.

Salad

375g block firm tofu

30ml rice syrup

50g coconut butter

50ml tamari

100g baby spinach

1 medium carrot

4 radishes

1 bunch broccolini or 1 head of broccoli

50g pepitas

Dressing

¼ cup Shiro miso

40g ginger

juice of 1 lemon

20ml toasted sesame oil

¼ cup boiling water

Cut the tofu into slices no thicker than 1cm. In a heavy-based pan, heat the coconut oil and then fry the tofu until crisp on both sides. Allow it to cool for a minute on a chopping board and then slice again into strips about 1cm wide. Place in a baking dish and pour the tamari and rice syrup evenly over the tofu. Allow it to sit and soak up the flavours while you get everything else ready. You may like to keep it warm in the oven at about 120°C.

Place the miso and boiling water in a jar and stir until smooth. Grate the ginger on the fine side of the grater and squeeze the juice out of it into the jar. (Don't throw out the grated part – you can use that in a curry or dahl.) Add the lemon juice and sesame oil, then put the lid on the jar and give it a good shake.

Slice the broccolini or broccoli into small pieces and steam for 4–5 minutes.

Peel the carrot, then grate or julienne. Slice the radish into very fine half-moons. Wash the baby spinach and dry in a salad spinner.

Combine the vegetables in a salad bowl and gently mix in half the dressing. Serve onto plates and then add tofu and finish with more dressing.

Dry-toast the pepitas in a heavy-based pan and sprinkle over salad to garnish.

Coconut quinoa porridge with banana & black sesame seeds

By Amy Crawford

www.theholisticingredient.com

Serves 2

The fibre, potassium, vitamin C and B6 content in **bananas** all support heart health. Studies have shown that those who consume more potassium have a lower risk of heart disease, along with decreased risk of stroke and kidney stones.

1 banana, mashed

1 cup coconut milk, fresh or canned

1 cup water

2/3 cup quinoa, uncooked

2 vanilla beans, seeded

2 tbsp chia seeds

1 tbsp black sesame seeds

Pinch of sea salt

Rinse the quinoa well under running water. Add quinoa, coconut milk, water, chia seeds, seeds of the vanilla beans and salt to a medium saucepan. Bring to the boil over medium heat. Reduce heat and simmer with lid on for 10–12 minutes or until the quinoa has a slight chew. Remove from heat and allow to stand for 2 minutes with lid on. Stir through the mashed banana and sesame seeds. Divide into two bowls, serve immediately.

WEEK TWO

Explore the breath

Deepen your focus

*'No valid plans for the future can be made by those
who have no capacity for living now.'*
Alan Watts

How was your first week of meditation?

Did you manage to meditate every day?

If you missed a day, don't be hard on yourself. Just get back on track this week.

I've been meditating for many years but there are still days when I feel like it's something I need to tick off the to-do list. On some days, particularly when I'm in the middle of a big project, it can feel hard to put even ten minutes aside for meditation practice.

Can you relate?

The driven voice in my head often tries to convince me that meditation is a waste of time. Some days it's an extremely compelling voice, but when I manage to identify the self-sabotaging thoughts that are connected with it, I'm able to reconnect with my practice and experience the enormous benefits.

When I sit to meditate on a challenging day, I immediately notice the tightness in my chest and throat and the underlying agitation of my stress. I notice my mind spewing out to-do lists in a way that urges me to get up and do things. Then I realise what is happening. *Ah, agitation is here.* By the end of my meditation session, I feel my chest open up, my breath flow more easily, my belly soften, and then my whole being settles back into a feeling of calm and ease.

It's often during the times when we are most stressed and busy that meditation drops off our daily routine, even though we know it is *exactly* the thing that would help us. It's an interesting catch-22 in which we can find ourselves resisting the very thing we need. John O'Donohue, the Irish poet and philosopher, reflected on this phenomenon, explaining:

> Stress is a perverted relationship with time, so that rather than being a subject of your own time, you become its target and victim, so that at the end of the day you probably haven't had a true moment for yourself to relax, and just be.

While stress contracts time, meditation expands it, and regularly sprinkling mindfulness into our busy lives is a way to create more space. I'm always surprised by the positive effect that just one minute of mindful breathing can have during a really busy day.

According to the research, the way we *perceive* stress has a large impact on how it affects us. The term 'stress' was coined in 1936 by Hungarian endocrinologist Hans Selye, and was defined as 'the non-specific response of the body to any demand for change'. He described two types of stress. The good stress he called '*eustress*', from the Greek prefix *eu* (good), a stress associated with feeling challenged but not overwhelmed, which fuels our performance. *Eustress* is frequently related to the state of 'flow' described by Mihaly Csikszentmihalyi in his book *Flow*. This is a state of complete absorption in the moment, where we lose a sense of time and space as we merge fully with the activity we are doing. 'Flow is a state of enjoyment that appears at the boundary between boredom and anxiety, when the challenges are just balanced with a person's capacity to act.'

In contrast, the bad stress, which Selye termed '*distress*', arises when we feel challenged by something we believe we don't have the resources to manage, and ultimately leads to anxiety and depression. Selye explains, 'It is not stress that kills us, it is our reaction to it.' One person's *eustress* might be another person's *distress*. It is the way we perceive challenges that determines if they will be experienced as *eustress* or *distress*.

In her book *The Upside of Stress*, health psychologist Kelly McGonigal emphasises this point through highlighting a significant research study from the University of Wisconsin-Madison. This study, involving twenty-nine thousand people over eight years, revealed that it was the individual's perception of stress that impacted their health far more than the stress itself. Those who believed the stress in their lives was harmful to their health were more negatively affected by stress, and consequently had shorter lives. Mindfulness meditation helps us relate to stress more effectively, giving us a better capacity to recognise it and then respond before it spirals out of control.

Many of us are living with chronic stress or 'distress', and this is having a serious impact on our bodies. Our stress response – or 'fight–flight response' – is a reflex that evolved thousands of years ago to protect us from physical threats. From an evolutionary perspective, it's what saved our lives when we were confronted by predators. However, while the changes triggered in our body during the fight–flight response are protective in the short term, they can be detrimental if overused. These changes are all aimed at creating as much energy as possible so we can literally fight the physical predator or run away. Glucose, the body's main source of energy, gets shifted out of storage from the liver and muscles, and it fills the bloodstream. Our heart rate and breathing rate increase to help pump energy and oxygen around the body more effectively. We turn off all of our non-critical systems such as digestion (the reason our mouth goes dry under stress), growth and reproduction in order to preserve energy for our muscles. The brain gets more blood-flow, allowing increased focus and memory so that we can remember the potential threat and learn from our experiences.

This system evolved for short, infrequent physical crises – like the occasional lion or other predator. But these days it's activated many times a day in response to psychosocial stressors such as fights with our loved ones or looming work deadlines. In addition to external stressors, the fight–flight response can also be triggered purely by our own imagination. Our worries or future concerns, negative thoughts and upsetting memories can all activate this response. What's going on in the mind impacts the body, and when our stress response is frequently switched on, it becomes more dangerous to us than the stressors themselves.

Chronic stress, or distress, leads to an increased risk of diabetes, heart attacks and several psychological illness including anxiety and depression (to name just a few of the potential negative impacts). It's known to damage cells in parts of the brain, especially the hippocampus, which is associated with memory and learning. This in part explains why children who grow up in abusive environments often have learning difficulties.

Stress and the Type A personality style

A link between stress and illness was famously uncovered in a busy cardiology clinic in San Francisco in the 1950s. Two cardiologists by the names of Dr Meyer Friedman and Dr Ray Rosenman noticed they were spending a lot of money on reupholstering the chairs in their waiting room. The upholsterer had remarked in passing that he'd never seen chairs that were worn down so quickly in a medical clinic.

Many years later, Dr Friedman recognised that a disproportionate number of his patients who'd had heart attacks were chronically stressed, competitive and driven CEOs. He decided to explore whether there was any scientific evidence to support the connection between their heart attacks and their behaviours and personality traits. Through his research he discovered that there was a pattern of behaviour that significantly increased the risk of heart attacks, which he termed 'Type A Behaviour'. People following this pattern were driven, ambitious, impatient, prone to reactive outbursts of anger and had a chronic sense of urgency. It was only in retrospect that Dr Friedman recalled his upholsterer's observation, and realised that his worn-out waiting-room chairs were thanks to these 'Type A' patients who were literally 'on the edge of their seats' all the time, impatient to see their doctor and get back to work. In fact they were suffering a stress syndrome that Dr Friedman later termed the 'hurry sickness'.

It's not only high-powered CEOs who are affected, of course. So many of us are trying to juggle the varied demands of life, and are living a version of this time-pressured existence – and it's literally wearing out our bodies.

Although meditation can't overcome the excessive influence of stress in our lives, it can help us actively switch our nervous systems from a state of stress to calm, which does have proven health benefits. Interestingly, you can notice this shift in the nervous system taking place while you meditate. Pay attention to the physical signs that indicate the 'rest and digest' (parasympathetic nervous system) being activated with an increase in gurgling bowel sounds (a sign of increased digestion) and a slowing down of the breath.

These physical signs are an indication of what Herbert Benson, a Harvard-trained physician, famously described as the 'relaxation response'. In his book *The Relaxation Revolution*, he describes it as the opposite of the 'fight-or-flight' response, characterised by the following symptoms:

- Decreased metabolism, heart rate, blood pressure and rate of breathing.
- A decrease or 'calming' in brain activity, but with an increase in attention and decision-making functions of the brain.
- Changes in gene activity that are the opposite to those associated with stress.

Mindfulness meditation activates this relaxation response, helping us to switch from fight-or-flight mode to a more restorative, relaxed state.

However, the power of meditation stretches even further than calming our nervous system. When Benson's colleague Sara Lazar, one of the world's leading neuroscientists, investigated the impact of meditation on the brain, she found some fascinating results.

After eight weeks of meditation, the amygdala, the stress centre of the brain, was reduced in volume, which implied a reduction in its activity. We know that people who suffer generalised anxiety disorders have amygdalas that are larger in volume than the non-anxious population, so this promising finding supports the possibility of mindfulness as an anxiety-reducing practice. The study also suggested there was an increase in the size of the hippocampus, an area of the brain responsible for memory and learning, which is usually *reduced* in volume and function by stress. This suggests that meditation is an effective tool for managing both the short-term and long-term effects of stress.

Anxiety currently affects about one in fourteen people worldwide. A systematic review conducted by Chen et al in 2012 revealed that meditation training alleviated symptoms of anxiety in approximately 70 per cent of the studies reviewed.

So as you continue your daily meditation practice this week, use the science to stay motivated.

Last week we spent time connecting with our senses to become more aware of the body and our immediate environment, and we explored some practices to bring mindfulness into everyday life. This week, we will start to develop focus and explore the connection between mind and body through the guided mindfulness of breath meditation. You'll discover how you can use breath to monitor your stress levels and also actively use it to calm yourself down when you're under pressure. Along with the daily guided meditation, you'll also find daily mindfulness exercises that will support you in deepening your focus at home and at work, while also bringing attention to how you can nourish yourself amidst the demanding pace of life.

Understanding the breath

People often wonder how they should breathe during meditation – through their mouth or their nose? It's best to just allow the breath to be as natural as possible, and not to focus too much on how you are breathing. However, during other times of the day, take a moment to notice if you're a nose breather or a mouth breather, as there is some interesting science around the benefits of nose breathing.

In *The Oxygen Advantage*, by world-renowned breathing expert

Patrick McKeown, ear nose and throat specialist Dr Marrs Cottle explains that the human nose is responsible for thirty functions. It filters the air and warms it, but it's also responsible for the release of a gas in the nasal cavity called nitric oxide. Although nitric oxide is a toxic pollutant in the external world, it actually has a positive impact on our breath and health. This gas sterilises the air as it moves into the lungs, opens up the airways and helps release more oxygen from the lungs into the blood, in effect making our breathing more efficient. Nitric oxide is produced at different sites in the body, but if you breathe through your nose you get fifty times more nitric oxide delivered to the lungs than if you were to breathe through the mouth.

We are all born nose-breathers, but as we grow into adulthood many of us become mouth-breathers, which leads to a greater risk of sleep apnoea and reduced energy and fatigue. The Buteyko method, created in the 1950s by Russian scientist Dr Konstantin Pavlovich Buteyko, is a way of breathing that has helped asthma sufferers experience fewer symptoms and has been used with athletes to improve their performance. The gist of the Buteyko method is to breathe through your nose and breathe less. Similarly, Chinese philosopher Lao Tzu said that 'the perfect person breathes as if he is not breathing'.

As you settle into the breath meditation each day this week, you'll notice that as the body calms down, the breath settles too and becomes very subtle – sometimes nearly undetectable. This week pay particular attention to how the breath changes during meditation.

More Resources

Read: Patrick McKeown's *The Oxygen Advantage*

Day One

MINDFULNESS OF BREATH MEDITATION

'If you have time to breathe, you have time to meditate.'
Ajahn Chah

Just like astronomers who need to rest their telescopes on stable ground in order to discover new aspects of the universe, we need to train our minds to be more focused and stable so we can see the many thought patterns that lead to our stress and suffering.

This week we move to the new guided breath meditation (which you'll find online at **www.mindlifeproject.com/book**). As you practise this meditation every day this week, there are three crucial words that will help you stay focused: **relax**, **release**, and **return**. These simple instructions will help you manage the inevitable distraction of the mind.

When you notice you've become lost in thinking, the first step is to **relax your body.** Often when we get pulled into our mind we become physically tense without realising it. The second step is to

release the thoughts. Imagine the thought is a helium balloon in your hands, and you're simply opening your grasp. You can also use each exhalation to release the thoughts, letting them go with each outbreath. The final step is to **return your attention** to the sensations of the breath, your anchor. These three words will remind you what you need to do to stay focused when faced with the constant challenge of a wandering mind.

Your breath is a reliable anchor for your attention because it's with you all the time, and it has powerful calming effects on the mind that have been utilised for millennia. As long as we're alive, we will breathe. Consciously bringing attention to the breath is a simple way to bring ourselves back to the present moment.

Your breath is a reference point that helps you recognise when the mind has wandered. Each time you notice that your thoughts have been pulled away from the breath and you bring them back, you are having a mindful moment. It's the act of bringing the mind back over and over again that will, over time, bring focus and clarity into your life.

Imagine that each time you catch the mind wandering and bring it back to the breath, you've completed a dumbbell lift for your brain. Just as strengthening muscle requires that you work against resistance in order to grow, strengthening the mind's capacity to focus requires that you work against the resistance of distraction.

So try your best to do the breath meditation every day of this week. If you are wanting extra mindfulness practice, you can also go back to the body scan or sound meditation from last week and add this to your daily practice. You can keep track of your observations and reflections in *The Happiness Plan* meditation journal (which can be downloaded from the resource page **www.mindlifeproject.com/book**).

MINDFULNESS OF BREATH GUIDANCE

Purpose

1. As with the previous meditations, the purpose here is to train the attention to stay in the present moment. Remember that although it's an added bonus to feel calmer while we meditate, it's not the primary purpose of this practice.
2. Our training is about learning how to be more aware in daily life, so that we're better at meeting the challenges in our lives with wisdom and resilience.

The practice

1. This practice is best done in the seated position, though you can do it lying down if you prefer. Sit in a comfortable chair and make sure your back is supported if needed. You may also like to use a meditation cushion if you have one.
2. Make sure your feet are flat on the floor with your legs uncrossed.
3. Your back, neck and head should be upright, but relaxed and comfortably balanced.
4. Keep your hands comfortably placed on your thighs.
5. Once you are seated and have adjusted your body position, try to stay as still as possible – this helps to still the mind.

Tips

1. See if you can consciously let go of any concerns you have about the past or the future when you sit to meditate, reminding yourself that you can come back to your worries and plans after the practice.

2. It can be helpful to focus the mind by counting your breath either from one to five or one to ten. You can repeat the cycle as many times as feels helpful to settle the mind.

3. Count 'one' the moment you finish the inbreath but have not yet begun the outbreath. This means your attention rests on the sensation of the outbreath as it releases.

4. The purpose behind counting is to replace the many distracting involuntary thoughts we all have, with one intentional thought.

5. Another helpful technique to help us stay focused on the breath is to label the movement of the breath as the belly rises and falls. As the belly expands on the inbreath, silently note 'rising', and as the belly falls back on the outbreath, silently note 'falling'.

You can listen to the mindfulness of breath meditation by visiting www.mindlifeproject.com/book

A condensed transcript of the practice is included below in case you'd prefer to read it and guide yourself through.

Mindfulness of breath meditation guidance

1. As in the body scan, first bring awareness to the body.

2. Use each outbreath to release any areas that are particularly tight or tense, as though each outbreath helps to melt those areas and allows the body to soften.

3. Sense how the breath feels in this moment, noticing as it flows in and out of the body.

4. Take a deep breath in, and let it go slowly. Take another deep breath in, and let it go.

5. Allow the breath to settle into its natural rhythm, not trying to change it or control it in any way. Allow it to continue naturally, noticing wherever you sense its movements.

6. Notice how the breath feels in this moment: is it relaxed or restricted, short or long?

7. You'll notice that the mind will get distracted. Each time you realise that you've become distracted, let go of the thoughts and gently bring your attention back to the next inbreath.

8. Each time you notice that your attention has drifted, gently come back to the next breath, feeling the sensations in the body as the breath flows in and out, bringing an attitude of patience and gentleness towards yourself as you gently continue to return your attention to the breath.

9. Stay present to each moment, seeing if you can rest the attention on just one breath as it flows in and out.

10. Rest in stillness as the breath moves in and out.

11. As this practice comes to an end, remember that you can touch base with your breath at any moment to take a pause and bring some mindfulness into your day.

As you meditate each day this week, you may start to sense the way your breath changes in relation to your emotional state. This is because the breath is intimately linked to our nervous system: when we're stressed it becomes constricted, rapid and located more noticeably in the chest, and when we're relaxed it's slower, flows with greater ease and is felt more in the belly. See if this is true for you the next time you are stressed or relaxed.

Apart from being a sign of our overall state, we can actually use our breath to calm ourselves down. In highly stressful situations, we can settle the nervous system by lengthening the outbreath. This works because these deeper, longer exhalations massage our vagus nerve, which is in charge of the 'rest and digest', or parasympathetic nervous system. This branch of the nervous system slows our heart and breathing rate, and generally calms us down.

TODAY'S PRACTICE
Activate 'rest and digest'

Along with today's new guided meditation, you may like to experiment with using your breath to calm your nervous system through the 'rest and digest' breathing cycle. In this incidental mindfulness practice, try using the breath to activate the calming branch of your nervous system. This will balance out the chronically activated fight-or-flight response. You can do this by breathing **in for four counts, holding for two counts,** breathing **out for six counts, holding for two counts** and repeating this rhythm of breathing for two minutes. If you have a moment, you can try it out right now.

Try this practice a few times today and see what you discover.

Day Two

MINDFUL WORK

'Everybody agrees that no one pursuit can be successfully followed by a man who is preoccupied with many things ... since the mind, when distracted, takes in nothing very deeply.'
Seneca

How did you find the breath meditation?

When you're new to meditation you may discover that focusing on the breath feels uncomfortable, or even makes you a bit anxious. Don't worry – that's common. If this does happen, just silently label the experience with the words 'feeling tightness' or 'feeling anxious' and remind yourself that it is simply an unpleasant feeling that will pass. If it's too challenging to stay with this feeling, you can return to the guided sound meditation.

Touching base with the breath throughout your day, even if just for one minute, can be a helpful way to literally catch your breath. Our everyday life and particularly the outer world of work can become so demanding that we lose touch with ourselves. Mindfulness training helps us balance being and doing, and offers us a space to reconnect with our deeper selves amidst the pull of our busy world.

In his book *A Hidden Wholeness*, Parker Palmer explores this dance of 'being and doing', describing what he calls the 'work before the work'. He writes: 'Before I turn to my work in the world, I have inner work to do.'

Paradoxically, carving out time for regular stillness amplifies our creativity and offers access to a deeper source for the work and impact we hope to have in the world.

During an interview for Mindful in May, Tara Brach, leading meditation teacher and writer, shared her perspectives with me on how mindfulness can actually support more meaningful and impactful 'doing' in our lives:

> I actually think of mindfulness and meditation as the grounds of impactful activity that can make a real difference in the world. I sometimes think of Gandhi, who took a day off each week, no matter what, to pray and meditate. He'd get in touch with what he said was his wisest self. All of his actions would spring from his most clear and compassionate inner life. In the same way, if we take time to pause and reconnect, we are actually more in touch with our intelligence and with our heart. And then whatever activity it is – whether it's creative and in the arts, or serving other people, or mathematical – whatever we are doing, we are more aligned and more effective.

Another way in which mindfulness can support us in being more effective in our work is through the improved focus we develop.

Take a moment to reflect on these questions

- How often are you multitasking?
- Do you believe that multitasking is making you more efficient?
- What are your habits when it comes to working? Do you have strategies or practices that help you stay focused?

During my medical training, I remember the overwhelm I often felt during a busy hospital on-call shift. My pager beeped without a break, nurses constantly calling for urgent help. It was impossible to meet all of these emergencies at once, and so I learned the art of triage.

The key to triaging is remembering that there is always time to pause and breathe before you decide what action is required. The problem is that when you're feeling overwhelmed, the brain goes into fight-or-flight mode, bringing an inner sense of urgency.

In this anxious state, most of us automatically multi-task as a way of trying to manage the competing demands. However, there has been a huge amount of research done around the impact of multitasking on our brains and our effectiveness. Here are just a few findings:

- Multi-tasking has been demonstrated to reduce brain density in areas that control empathy and emotions (the anterior cingulate cortex).
- A study at the University of London found that subjects who multi-tasked experienced drops in their IQ comparable to someone who missed a night of sleep.
- A famous study at Stanford led by Clifford Nass revealed that multi-taskers were not as effective at remembering and learning new information.

That's where mindfulness really comes to the rescue. It won't necessarily stop you from getting overwhelmed, but it will help you *know* that you're overwhelmed, so that you can take a moment to pause and prioritise. The increased self-awareness that develops through a regular mindfulness practice helps you recognise changing states of mind more quickly and manage them more effectively.

TODAY'S PRACTICE
Mindfulness at Work

Today, experiment with this simple way to stay focused, manage the overwhelm and move from multi-tasking to mono-tasking in order to maximise your efficiency.

1. Choose one task that you will focus on during the set time period.
2. Get a plain piece of paper and pen and have them by your computer or workspace.
3. Set a timer for thirty minutes.
4. Set an intention to stay focused for your set period of time.
5. When you notice yourself getting distracted or feel an urge to move to another task (such as checking your email), simply note down the task or distraction on the paper and bring your attention back to the task you intend to focus on. At the end of the thirty minutes you can review your list and set your next priority.

For further time management and productivity hacks, consider downloading a pomodoro app. The Pomodoro Technique was created in the 1980s by Francesco Cirillo, and it involves dividing your work time into twenty-five-minute increments of focused attention with regular breaks in between. This technique helps bring more mindful awareness to the way we work, and supports efficiency and focus. There are several apps available to help you practise the Pomodoro Technique, many of them free.

ARE YOU AN INCESSANT LIST–MAKER DURING MEDITATION?

When you notice you're in 'doing' mode and feel agitated or on edge, set a timer for three minutes before you meditate to 'brain dump' and get your to-do list down on paper. This can give you a sense of greater freedom and mental space before you sit down to meditate. Of course your mind won't necessarily stop planning, but it may reduce the intensity of the list-making and allow you to settle into the practice with ease. Once your meditation is finished you can come back to your to-do list with increased calm and clarity.

More Resources
Download: Pomodoro Keeper app
Read: David Rock's *Your Brain at Work*

Day Three

MINDFUL TECHNOLOGY

*'The difference between technology and slavery is that slaves
are fully aware that they are not free.'*
Nassim Nicholas Taleb

As you continue to train your brain towards greater focus through the mindfulness of breath meditation, it's worth also considering how you can reduce the distractions in your environment to support more focus in your life.

With invisible umbilical cords connecting us to our devices 24/7, staying focused is becoming increasingly difficult. Our attention buzzes around with the restlessness of a mosquito, fluttering between emails, Facebook, Twitter and text messages. Many of us are suffering from what Dr Edward Hallowell, a psychiatrist specialising in ADHD, calls 'Attention Deficit Trait'. He describes it as 'a condition induced by modern life, in which you've become so busy attending to so many inputs and outputs that you become increasingly distracted, irritable, impulsive, restless and, over the long term, underachieving'.

We need to reflect on our relationships with technology, not just for the sake of improving our productivity, but also in relation to our health. Linda Stone, a technology thought leader and ex-Microsoft researcher discovered a condition she described as 'email apnoea', a pattern of breath-holding that occurs while emailing. It's a condition similar to sleep apnoea, which causes disturbed breathing during sleep. The problem with holding your breath is that it activates your stress response, leading to increased cortisol levels that can have a negative effect on your health. So becoming more mindful of our relationship with technology is going to improve our general wellbeing as well as our focus.

TODAY'S PRACTICE
Mindful Reflection

As a society, the constant distraction of technology is also affecting the health and safety of children under our care. In 2007 the iPhone was released, and according to the US Centre for Disease Control and Prevention (CDC), over the following three years nonfatal injuries to children under five increased by twelve per cent. Craig Palsson, professor of economics at Yale University, investigated whether there was a link between the two. In 2014 he published an alarming paper entitled 'That Smarts! Smartphones and Child Injuries', which revealed a connection: technology was increasingly distracting parents, and by extension impacting on the wellbeing of their children.

If we wish to remain healthy, happy and clear-minded, we need to upgrade our 'inner technology' to meet the demands of our increasingly complex, hyperconnected world. Mindfulness can significantly help with addictions ranging from smoking to social media, and it can help us manage the distractions and urges that constantly threaten our capacity to focus.

Take a moment to reflect on these questions to assess your level of addiction to social media. These are the same questions I used to ask many of my patients to determine whether they had addiction disorders, taken from a list of criteria in the *Diagnostic Statistical Manual* (DSM).

- Are you are spending increasing amounts of time on social media and often longer than you intend to be using it?
- Have you wanted to stop using social media but found you were unable to?
- Do you spend a lot of time on social media?
- Do you have strong urges or cravings to use social media that are hard to resist?
- Do you repeatedly find that some of your major tasks or responsibilities are being interrupted by your social media use (i.e. getting distracted when you should be working)?
- Do you continue to use social media despite it having a negative impact on areas of your life (i.e. staying up late at night and not getting enough sleep, having a child or partner point out your use of social media, using social media while driving)?
- Have you stopped or reduced doing things that you previously did (work, recreation or social) because of your social media use?
- Do you use social media repeatedly even when it puts you

or those around you in danger (i.e. while driving or in the playground with your child)?

- Have you continued use of social media despite knowing that it's causing problems in your life (either physical or psychological)?
- Do you need to use social media more often to get a sense of satisfaction?
- Do you feel withdrawal symptoms after being disconnected from social media that can be relieved by using it?

If you answered yes to two or three questions it is likely that you're mildly addicted, four to five indicates a moderate addiction, and six to seven indicates a severe addiction.

If you suspect that you may be addicted to technology, try these steps as a way of gaining some space:

1. **Set an intention**

   Set an intention around changing your behaviour in relation to technology and think about practical steps you can take to make it more difficult to access. Consider taking the social media apps off your phone, or commit to sleeping without your mobile in the bedroom (even for just a few nights to see what effect it has).

2. **Recognise**

   The next time you feel the urge to check social media, take a pause. Recognise that you are caught in craving. Count to ten before continuing to use it, as a way of interrupting the urge for long enough to allow it to naturally pass.

3. **Investigate**

   When we crave something, there's often an uncomfortable emotion or feeling that's present which we are trying to avoid. Take a moment to bring the attention to your body. Sense any emotions or feelings that are present (agitation, stress, loneliness, boredom). Once you identify the emotion, silently label it to yourself. This brings more mindful awareness to your current state and may lead you closer to the underlying issue that might be driving the urges.

4. **Unhook**

   Mindfulness allows you to consciously notice what is happening *as* it is happening – and pause before you act on your urges. In this way it helps disrupt automatic habits and addiction loops, and allows new habit pathways to form.

Don't forget to meditate today, using the guided meditation practice at **www.mindlifeproject.com/book**. It's a healthy habit that will counter the distracting forces of technology in your life.

Day Four

MINDFUL SLEEPING
AND WAKING

'Every morning we are born again. What we do
today is what matters most.'
The Buddha

Along with training our attention through mindfulness, developing focus also requires that we look after our general wellbeing. Getting enough sleep is crucial to our capacity to focus, think clearly and generally be well.

Sleep deprivation can significantly impair our mental performance and, in some situations, put us at risk of accidents. Investigations into the 1979 nuclear accident at Three Mile Island and the 1986 nuclear meltdown at Chernobyl revealed that sleep deprivation was a significant factor in both accidents. Even if you're not dealing with radioactive material, chances are there are many moments in your day when alertness and awareness are crucial.

As a doctor working on-call, often in a sleep-deprived state, I would worry about my own impaired mental performance. A colleague once told me that one night during her shift she found herself writing the contents of her dreams into a patient's file. Although at first the story made me laugh, it was a frightening reminder of the very real impact of sleep deprivation.

Even without working night shifts, many of us are suffering sleep deprivation thanks to our mobile phones. Given that the last thing many of us do before we try to sleep is check our phones, or collapse into bed directly from a computer screen, it's not surprising insomnia is an increasing problem.

At night, the light from our devices throws our circadian rhythm completely out of whack, and science has proven that blue light – the light emitted from our devices – actually suppresses melatonin (a hormone that influences our circadian rhythm and supports sleep).

A few tips for getting a better night's sleep

Try to reduce your exposure to blue light at least an hour before bed (mobile phone, computer and tablet screens). If your work requires you to be near screens at night, you can try out blue-light blocker glasses.

If you are prone to thinking and planning while trying to go to sleep, take five minutes to 'brain-dump' in the evening. Write down all of the things that are on your mind and the things you need to do the next day. This won't get rid of all your to-dos, as the mind is a brilliant thought generator, but at least it will give you a finite time and space to create some lists for yourself and get your thoughts out of your head and down on paper.

Do the breath meditation (or one of the other guided meditations in this book) just before you are planning to go to sleep. This time, if you fall asleep while you are doing the practice, it's an added benefit.

You can also bring mindfulness to the moment you wake up in the morning. Tomorrow morning as soon as you wake up, take a moment to reflect on these questions:

- What is the first thing you do immediately after you wake up?
- What kinds of thoughts are you thinking, and how do these colour the way you feel and move into your day?

Rather than wallowing in thoughts about how tired you are, which can exhaust you before you've even started your day, the moment you wake up, actively shift your attention to things you can be grateful for.

To help myself wake up more mindfully, I created a morning practice called the **'ten-by-three wakeup'**, and I quickly noticed how powerfully it affected the rest of my day. It shifted my attention in a way that made my body feel lighter and helped me step into the day with more energy. As I brought more conscious awareness to how I felt each morning, it also became more obvious that I needed to start getting to bed earlier at night to avoid always waking up feeling exhausted.

Mindfulness makes our patterns more obvious and gives us more insight into our own lives.

This practice takes less than a minute, but can have a big impact on your mood.

TODAY'S PRACTICE
The Ten-By-Three Wake-Up

This mindful morning practice is a quick and powerful energy shifter, and an easy way to start your day with presence and gratitude.

1. When you first wake up in the morning, take a moment to sense how you are feeling: Rested? Tired? Lazy? Energetic?

2. Bring awareness to your body, and more specifically to the feeling of your breath.

3. Before you do anything else (like check your phone!), count ten breaths as they move in and out of the body and make sure that as you are counting, you actually feel the sensations of the breath in your body, allowing your mind to be free from any concerns about the day to come. If you lose count and get distracted, simply begin again when you notice you've lost count.

4. After counting the breaths, drop the counting and bring to mind three things you are grateful for.

5. Get out of bed and start your day with a positive, appreciative attitude.

WAKE UP ON THE RIGHT SIDE OF THE BED

What does your morning routine look like? Take a few
moments to reflect on any changes you'd like to make.

How could you start your morning in a more conscious way by
engaging in an activity that improves your sense of wellbeing
and mindfulness? Perhaps you could connect with your body
through a short stretching session, or allow yourself time to
sit and eat breakfast rather than rushing out the door?

Notice how these small adjustments affect you.

Day Five

EXPLORE BEGINNER'S MIND

'Our goal should be to live life in radical amazement, get up in the morning and look at the world in a way that takes nothing for granted. Everything is phenomenal; everything is incredible; never treat life casually. To be spiritual is to be amazed.'
Abraham Joshua Heschel

As we approach the end of Week Two, it's easy to become a little complacent about your meditation practice.

One key attitude in the practise of mindfulness is the 'beginner's mind'. This is the ability to bring a freshness to your experience, seeing things 'as if for the first time', which allows you to drop your assumptions, ideas and desires, and instead be completely open to your experience. I'm often reminded of this quality by my two-year-old daughter. When I took her to the snow for the first time, she became completely absorbed in her exploration. In mindfulness we're invited to bring this quality of attention and curiosity to our meditation practice. Through beginner's mind, we stay engaged and alert in our practice, and in our lives.

Through beginner's mind, the fog of 'ordinary' starts to lift, and we see our lives with freshness and delight. Rather than seeing what we *think* is there, we see what is *actually* there. This new way of seeing opens us to new possibilities as we step out of our self-limiting assumptions, beliefs and habits.

Imagine how bringing a beginner's mind to just one day of your life could change how you experience your family, friends, work and the many aspects of your day.

Life can get so busy that it's easy to take the people closest to us for granted, and not be truly present to them. The 'beginner's mind' that we practise through mindfulness reminds us to wake up and experience the preciousness of those around us.

Beginner's mind helps me cut through the sometimes monotonous daily routine of motherhood and experience precious moments where my full presence meets my daughter's, and I'm moved to tears. Looking into the deep, dark-brown eyes of this little girl, I'm overwhelmed by her purity and innocence, and the complete miracle of her existence. I'm aware that she is still very close to an original, non-separate consciousness that connects all living things; the incomprehensible intelligence of life is peering out at me, the intelligence that has transformed itself from an embryo into a complex human being.

Children are a potent source of mindfulness. These days my daughter is my main teacher as I navigate the extended, not-so-silent mindfulness meditation retreat that is motherhood. Some nights after book time, I lie with her and we meditate together. I've introduced her to the concept of meditation, experimenting with how much she can understand of the practice. We watch a teddy move up and down on her belly as she breathes, and she giggles with delight. Then we do a few *Om* chants together – there is nothing religious in this chant, we're just enjoying the sound of singing in unison. We chant, 'Om, Om, Om,' as we gaze into each other's eyes. To enjoy this stillness with a toddler feels almost holy, a rare moment, as we manage to maintain eye contact for a few minutes.

In these moments it often occurs to me that my partner, my parents, all the people in my life and the strangers I walk past in the street are also mysterious living, breathing expressions of consciousness. Yet somehow, as we get older, it gets harder to maintain this wonder about one another, this beginner's mind. Somehow the complete innocence of my daughter seems to be a direct line to presence and pure consciousness. It's this exact quality of being that we try to return to through the practice of meditation.

Today, as well as the daily meditation, integrate mindfulness into your day by activating the beginner's mind when interacting with people in your life.

TODAY'S PRACTICE
Explore Beginner's Mind

An interesting way to experiment with beginner's mind is to activate curiosity and step into greater presence during conversations and interactions with friends, family and workmates.

When you are interacting, notice the tone of voice and facial expressions of the other person. Watch the light and shadow on their face, notice eye contact or lack of eye contact, the colour of their eyes. Pay attention to these people in your life as if you have never met them before.

Aside from paying close visual attention, ask questions from a place of curiosity rather than from your own specific agenda, and discover new stories from people who have been in your life for decades. When you're with family members, a partner or a friend, remind yourself that even though you think you know everything about this person, you actually don't. Ask them a question you've never asked them before and try to uncover something new.

Some conversation-starting questions

- What is your earliest memory?
- What is something I don't know about you?
- What is a positive memory from your childhood?
- What was it like being [insert any age]?
- How do you think you have changed from the person you were [insert number] years ago?
- What is something you've learned lately that really surprised you?
- What is a piece of advice you were given that had a positive impact on your life?
- What is one thing you would really like to do before you die?
- What's the biggest lesson life has taught you?

Day Six

CONNECT WITH WHAT MAKES YOU FEEL ALIVE

'The most regretful people on earth are those who felt the call to creative work, who felt their own creative power restive and uprising, and gave to it neither power nor time.'
Mary Oliver

How is your meditation practice going? Did you manage to find the time to practise yesterday?

As I mentioned earlier in this book, it was while sitting in meditation that I was inspired by an idea that ended up transforming my life and career.

As you continue to regularly practise mindfulness, you'll discover its ability to help expand your creativity, which is an essential ingredient for your happiness and flourishing.

The word inspiration comes from the Latin *inspirare*, 'to breathe in spirit'. So as you continue with the breath meditation, focus on how you could bring greater creativity into your life or work, to feel more energised and alive.

Over the past few years I've been on a mission of unlearning self-protective habits and relearning how to be comfortable with taking more risks and developing my creativity.

Going to medical school taught me a lot of worthwhile things, but it also seemed to gradually extinguish my creative and entrepreneurial tendencies. We were learning to accurately diagnose so that we could precisely treat and save lives. Mistakes could be devastating, so there wasn't a lot of room for creativity.

As I travelled deeper down the path of specialisation into psychiatry, I felt myself becoming more and more constricted by the rules, both spoken and unspoken, and less able to take risks and innovate within the system. There was a sense of having my creativity stifled by some invisible force.

I wasn't alone. Many of my doctor friends were talented musicians, artists and writers who were living double lives, barely managing to keep their creativity alive in between the demanding hours of medical work. Writer and social researcher Brené Brown warns about the toxicity of stifled creativity:

'Unexpressed creativity is not benign, it turns to grief and judgment.'

The grief that came from 'unexpressed creativity' was something I was familiar with.

I loved art at school. I remember walking down the corridors on my way to physics and peering into the art room, looking at the canvases in progress. I wished I could spend my school days painting and exploring the world of imaginative expression. However, based on the well-meaning advice of those around me, I internalised the idea that I wasn't creative enough to pursue an artistic vocation. It took a while to see that my 'I love art, but I'm not creative' story was a psychological prison stifling my creativity.

Creativity is a fundamental life force, and as the world becomes a more complex and challenging place, creativity is going to be an essential skill for our survival as a species.

Whether it's a desire to play music, paint, find creative solutions at work, or be a more creative parent or partner, meditation is a powerful practice that can help us overcome the barriers to our highest creative potential.

One common barrier to creativity is a lack of space and time for just 'being' rather than 'doing'. In an era of information and technology overload, meditation creates an oasis of quiet, giving the mind space to decompress. Although meditation is not about actively trying to make something happen, ripples of thought and emotion can creatively collide and result in innovative ideas and solutions to difficult problems we face. As Einstein famously stated, 'We cannot solve our problems with the same thinking we used when we created them.' Mindfulness meditation cultivates an open state of mind, which is a prerequisite to bringing about an alternative perspective.

Another obstacle to our creativity is the inner critic, which stops us from taking creative risks for fear of humiliation. Our internal voice tries to protect us from perceived danger, but in the process inhibits us from trying new things for fear that we'll fail. Mindfulness helps us recognise these inner dialogues for what they are: an obstacle between us and our deepest hopes and longings. Once we see this inner chatter, we can allow it to be there, label it as fear, and move forward despite its threats and provocations.

TODAY'S PRACTICE
A Mindful Reflection

Take a moment after your meditation today to reflect on these questions and journal your responses.

- Where in your life is your creativity being expressed?
- Where in your life is your creativity not being expressed?˙
- What creative longings do you have that you may not have acted upon because of fear?
- What are the inner and outer obstacles that prevent you from experiencing your creativity?
- What is one thing you could do this week at work or at home to nurture and encourage your creativity?

A powerful aspect of mindfulness practice is that it invites you to regularly take notice of how you are feeling. This opens up an opportunity to consider which aspects of your life need attention. It's through offering ourselves space that we can hear the whisper of what our soul needs to feel nourished and happy.

Parker Palmer likens the soul to a wild animal that we have to approach with gentleness. He writes:

The soul is like a wild animal – tough, resilient, savvy, self-sufficient, and yet exceedingly shy. If we want to see a wild animal, the last thing we should do is to go crashing through the woods, shouting for the creature to come out. But if we are willing to walk quietly into the woods and sit silently for an hour or two at the base of a tree, the creature we are waiting for may well emerge, and out of the corner of an eye we will catch a glimpse of the precious wildness we seek.

When we're feeling rushed and stressed out, we lose touch with those things that nourish us at a soul level. Taking time to be still and listen to what we need helps us sense what is missing in our lives, and allows us to make small adjustments that can often have a big impact on how we feel.

Whether you call it a soul or spirit, or simply a deep-set part of the psyche, we all have an internal aspect of ourselves that feels essential and vital. It's that part of ourselves that feels most alive as we watch a sunset or find ourselves surrounded by the vast beauty of nature. The loss of connection to our soul is a key contributor to so many of our psychological ailments.

Although medication can at times be lifesaving in helping people overcome episodes of depression or anxiety, in my training I've discovered that helping people reconnect with what makes them feel most alive can be a crucial ingredient in the healing process. Gabrielle Roth, dancer, musician and founder of 5rhythms global dance movement, highlights the powerful healing capacity that creativity and play can have in our lives in her book *Maps to Ecstasy*. She writes:

> In many shamanic societies, if you came to a shaman or medicine person complaining of being disheartened, dispirited, or depressed, they would ask one of four questions: When did you stop dancing? When did you stop singing? When did you stop being enchanted by stories? When did you stop finding comfort in the sweet territory of silence? Where we have stopped dancing, singing, being enchanted by stories, or finding comfort in silence is where we have experienced the loss of soul.

What nourishes you?

Write a list of the types of activities you engage in on a regular day and note down whether the activities are nourishing or depleting. Of course there are things we need to do each day that may feel depleting but which we can't change, such as driving to work in peak hour. However, look at the depleting activities and see if you can bring a sprinkle of creativity to them and work out how to make them more nourishing. For example, you might start listening to podcasts or audio books while you drive to work.

Take a look at the rest of your weekly schedule and factor in an extra-nourishing activity for each day.

- Turn the monotony of daily cooking into something novel by choosing a challenging or interesting new recipe.
- Read a poem each morning before you get out of bed to tap into creativity.
- Subscribe to a free music platform and explore new music by making your own playlist. Play the music at home to set a new atmosphere in the house.
- Bring your friends together over a pot-luck dinner and tap into greater connection in your life.
- Schedule a trip somewhere novel that you've been meaning to visit.

More Resources

Listen: *On Being* (podcast) with Krista Tippett
Read: Poetry by David Whyte or Rainer Maria Rilke
Cook: Recipes by www.deliciouslyella.com

Day Seven

TURNING CHALLENGES INTO OPPORTUNITIES FOR GROWTH

'If it weren't for my mind, my meditation would be excellent.'
Pema Chödrön

Over my years of teaching meditation, I have found that there is a common, limiting belief that gets in the way of people progressing with their practice, and that is the belief that they are a bad meditator.

The beliefs we carry through life can have a profound impact on our ability to grow and reach our full potential. Carol Dweck, Stanford University developmental psychologist, discovered two common beliefs, or mindsets, that have a profound effect on our potential for growth and our ability to learn from challenges. People with a **fixed mindset** believe that their talents, capacities and intelligence are fixed qualities. There's a sense that they have a set aptitude or skillset and that the person they are is who they'll always be. In contrast, people with a **growth mindset** believe that their capacity, skills and intelligence can be developed through hard work, strong strategies and support from others. They are always striving to learn and grow and don't get too stressed out by failure. Rather, they see it as a sign of their growth.

With practice we can change our mindset towards a growth mindset, and turn challenges into opportunities for growth. In a conversation I had with Carol Dweck she shared:

> In many studies where, for example, we follow students over school transitions, in the end those with a growth mindset do better in terms of their grades. When we teach students the growth mindset, every time they stretch outside of their comfort zone and do new and hard things, the neurons in their brains form stronger connections and they get smarter. Also, researchers at Berkeley have done a very impressive series of studies showing that when you teach the growth mindset to people they become more creative on the tasks that you give them.

TODAY'S PRACTICE
Adopt a Growth Mindset

In order to shift from a fixed mindset to a growth mindset we need to bring sharp attention to our inner voice. Here are three steps that Carol suggests to support the development of a growth mindset.

1. **Recognise 'fixed mindset' thoughts**
   This is particularly important when you're moving out of your comfort zone and challenging yourself to do something new. Look for doubting thoughts, such as, 'I don't think I'm smart enough.'

2. **Recognise that you have a choice**

   How you interpret challenges, setbacks or criticism is a choice. You can bring a fixed mindset to challenges and decide that you can't do it because you're not smart enough, or you can bring a growth mindset to life and decide that challenges or failures can be signs that you need to try new ways of approaching a problem or that you need to get more support to learn.

3. **Talk to your fixed mindset voice with a growth mindset**

   When facing challenges, failures or criticism, if you catch yourself falling into a fixed mindset, create a growth mindset response. A helpful way of generating this is to imagine what you might say to a close friend experiencing the same challenge or failure.

Carol also offers these helpful suggestions:

As you approach a challenge

The fixed mindset says ...	The growth mindset answers ...
'Are you sure you can do it? Maybe you don't have the talent.'	'I'm not sure I can do it now, but I think I can learn to with time and effort.'
'What if you fail – you'll be a failure'	'Most successful people had failures along the way.'
'This would have been easy if you really had talent.'	'That is so wrong. Basketball wasn't easy for Michael Jordan and science wasn't easy for Thomas Edison. They had a passion and put in tons of effort.'

A powerful word that can support us in developing a growth mindset is 'yet'. For instance, if a child says, 'I'm not good at maths,' you can add 'yet'. This reframing reminds children (and adults) that with more practice and support we all have the potential to grow.

Don't forget to do your daily meditation today, and remember to bring a growth mindset to the practice.

More Resources
Read: Carol Dweck's *Mindset*

Congratulations on completing

WEEK TWO

How has your meditation practice been this week? Have you managed to do the guided breath practice every day?

Hopefully you've explored bringing mindfulness to the way you work and you've scheduled in some activities that nourish and inspire you to create a happy balance between being and doing.

After two weeks of daily meditation, you may find yourself asking, is this actually working? Life is so busy, and it's important to critically assess whether what we are spending our time on is worthwhile. However, as I mentioned earlier in the book, the benefits of meditation are cumulative and don't happen immediately. Sometimes, it's only when we look backwards that we can assess how things have changed.

One of the biggest obstacles to experiencing the potentially transformative effects of mindfulness meditation is impatience.

In this time of immediate gratification, where answers to every question are at the tips of our fingers, it's hard for us to tolerate things that take time.

In his book *Zorba the Greek*, Nikos Kazantzakis shares a poignant story of his own impatience and the lesson he learned from nature.

I remember one morning when I discovered a cocoon in the back of a tree just as a butterfly was making a hole in its case and preparing to come out. I waited a while, but it was too long appearing and I was impatient. I bent over it and breathed on it to warm it. I warmed it as quickly as I could and the miracle began to happen before my eyes, faster than life. The case opened; the butterfly started slowly crawling out, and I shall never forget my horror when I saw how its wings were folded back and crumpled; the wretched butterfly tried with its whole trembling body to unfold them. Bending over it, I tried to help it with my breath, in vain.

Through this experience Nikos concludes, 'It is a mortal sin to violate the great laws of nature. We should not hurry, we should not be impatient, but we should confidently obey the rhythm of things.'

Take a moment to consider your own relationship to patience.

Are you as patient as you would like to be?

Where does impatience show up most noticeably in your life?

As you continue to practise meditating each day this week, notice the impatience that can arise in your meditation session. This can manifest as physical restlessness or impatient thoughts that urge you to get up and do all the things you need to do.

In many ways meditation is a type of detox process for the mind, where we are cleansing ourselves of the overstimulation that clouds our perception and makes us feel restless and on edge. If you've ever tried to wean yourself off caffeine or sugar, you'll know the strong cravings that you need to overcome as your body adapts to the changes. So too, when making meditation a regular habit, we are likely to feel impatience. It's a sign that the mind is detoxing from excessive stimulation and moving towards calm, clarity and focus. It's important to remember that no matter the quality of your meditation, what's most important is your intention and ability to meditate, whether you feel like it or not.

So reconnect with your intention and move into the next week with a commitment to meditate every day.

MIND FOOD

Feed your brain and nurture your mind

As you continue to strengthen your focus this week through the mindfulness of breath meditation, here are a few recipes that will help you nourish your mind so it functions at its best.

Very berry chocolate chia breakfast mousse

Amy Crawford
www.theholisticingredient.com
Serves 1

Raw **cacao** is one of the highest plant-based sources of magnesium, the most deficient mineral in those living in the Western world. Magnesium is important in converting glucose into energy to fuel the brain. It is also considered the highest antioxidant food on earth, a natural mood elevator and an antidepressant.

1 cup almond milk (or milk of choice)

¼ cup berries (I used frozen in the mousse)

3 tbsp chia seeds

1 tbsp good quality raw cacao (in my case, heaped)

1–2 heaped tablespoons Greek or natural yoghurt (or CoYo)

1 heaped tsp maca powder

2 tsp rice-malt syrup or Stevia to taste

Optional toppings: a dollop of yoghurt and fresh berries

Throw all ingredients into your blender/Thermomix and blend until smooth. I like mine really, really thick and smooth so I let it run for a minute or two. Given its lack of liquid, it will now be pretty thick. I pour mine into a glass and pop it into the fridge for twenty minutes to let the chia seeds soften (easier on your digestion).

Green 'pizza omelette'

Amy Crawford
www.theholisticingredient.com
Serves 1

Eggs are egg-ceptionally good for healthy brains and memory. Not only do they contain abundant folate, choline and vitamin B12, but the yolks of free-range hens are an important source of omega-3 fatty acids, which play a vital role in building the brain itself.

2 eggs
1 hefty handful of baby or English spinach
pinch of salt
½–1 cup of steamed vegetables
Goats cheese to sprinkle, optional
A few cherry tomatoes
1 tsp coconut oil

Pop a small oven-proof pan onto the stove on low-medium heat. Turn your grill on.

Meanwhile, blend your eggs, spinach and salt in your food processor/blender until smooth.

Melt the coconut oil in the pan. Pour the green goodness into the pan and cook as you would an omelette, but don't flip it over. When it looks almost ready to flip, sprinkle your steamed vegetables and goats cheese on top and leave for a couple of minutes to heat through. Place the pan under the grill for a couple of minutes or until the top is well-cooked and starting to brown.

Remove from the oven and sprinkle with fresh cherry tomatoes (I really love a little bit of rawness with my cooked food, where possible). Breakfast, lunch or dinner is served, in about ten minutes.

Kale, walnut & sun-dried tomato salad

Sun Hyland

www.neweartheating.com

Serves 4

Ever noticed how **walnuts** look similar to a human brain?
Considered the ultimate brain superfood, walnuts are replete
with omega-3 fatty acids, an essential fatty acid to keep the
brain functioning normally. Low omega-3 intake has been
linked to depression, so eat a fistful of walnuts and keep your
mind clear.

1 bunch Tuscan kale

⅛ purple cabbage

½ cup sundried tomatoes

100 g walnuts (activated if available)

1 cup alfalfa sprouts

30 ml apple cider vinegar

30 ml extra virgin olive oil

1 tsp salt

Wash the kale. Remove the stems and slice the kale very finely.
Do the same with the purple cabbage. Place in a bowl with the
salt and apple cider vinegar. Using your hands, mix the salt and
vinegar through the leaves and then 'massage' the vinegar into
the leaves for a minute or two. Allow to sit for at least an hour.

This is a form of 'quick pickling' or 'passive cooking' (cooking without heat), as cabbage and kale can be difficult to digest raw. Massaging the acid into the kale starts to break it down, allowing the Vitamin A and other nutrients contained therein to become more bioavailable.

Slice the sundried tomato as finely as you feel. I usually buy dried tomatoes and rehydrate and marinate them myself. To do this, soak 1 cup of dried tomatoes in 2 cups of boiled water for at least 1 hour. Drain in a fine mesh strainer (if you want them to keep for longer, leave them in the strainer over a bowl in the fridge overnight – this gets rid of almost all the moisture). Marinate the rehydrated tomatoes with ¼ cup olive oil, a splash of balsamic, a ½ teaspoon salt and a ½ teaspoon freshly cracked pepper.

Roughly chop the walnuts and add to the leaves along with the tomatoes, olive oil and sprouts.

This also makes a delicious warm side dish in the colder months: before you add the sprouts, gently heat everything else in a heavy pan with a little water.

WEEK THREE

Explore your thoughts

Be mindful of emotions

'Very little is needed to make a happy life; it is all within yourself, in your way of thinking.'

Marcus Aurelius

Congratulations!

You have now arrived at the halfway mark of the one-month Happiness Plan.

If you've managed to maintain your daily meditation practice, take a moment to really acknowledge your efforts.

If your practice has slipped, remember that you can start again at any moment.

During the years that I've been teaching mindfulness meditation, I've noticed how people often assume that unless they're doing twenty or thirty minutes of meditation a day, they're not really meditating properly. Of course, the more you meditate, the more you'll experience the benefits. However, for those who feel that meditating for half an hour each day is unrealistic, practising for ten or fifteen minutes a day with the guided meditations in this book is a good alternative. Remember, the key to experiencing the benefits of meditation is to practise regularly. Even just five or ten minutes of daily practice is more beneficial than squeezing in a longer session once or twice a week.

Tulku Urgyen Rinpoche, one of the greatest Tibetan meditation masters of the 20th-century, emphasised that there is value in practising meditation for **short periods, many times**. He acknowledged that in the modern world, even ten to fifteen minutes a day of meditation is a significant commitment and should not be underestimated in its potential to transform the mind.

This week we take the calm and focus that we've developed over the last two weeks and bring our attention to the complex and at times elusive world of our thoughts and emotions.

One of the biggest revelations that comes from mindfulness meditation is the new relationship we develop with our thoughts. This new perspective creates a sense of freedom and ease in our life as we become master of our own mind rather than a slave to its reactivity.

In mindfulness training we turn our attention towards thoughts themselves, making them the focus of our meditation and observing them as if they were little bubbles moving through the space of our mind. This practice highlights how often we get lost in habitual patterns of thinking, including judging, commenting, and thinking about what we like or dislike. We can discover how easy it is to get caught up in these habits of the mind without even realising this has happened. Mindfulness not only helps us see our thought patterns more clearly, but also helps us to release ourselves from the habitual thinking that increases our suffering.

Worry is one of the many negative thought patterns that increase our stress. The anxious mind gets caught in future thinking and obsessing about things that could go wrong, even though most of these things don't eventuate. As Mark Twain famously stated, 'I've had a lot of worries in my life, most of which never happened.' In regularly turning our attention inwards, and recognising that we can observe our thoughts rather than get lost in them, we discover that we actually have a choice about how we relate to them.

Along with making us more aware of our thoughts, mindfulness helps us understand and more effectively manage our emotions, and the relationship between the two. Exploring the research in this area, I've often puzzled over which comes first, the thought or the emotion.

Take a moment to reflect on this from your own experience. Do your emotions follow your thoughts or do your emotions lead to particular types of thinking? Do you feel sad because you've had thoughts that upset you, or do sad thoughts arise because you have experienced a sad feeling? It's not just a philosophical question. Understanding how thoughts and emotions are related is an important step in being able to manage them more effectively and reduce the negative impact they can have on us. According to Barbara Fredrickson, leading researcher in the field of emotions, it's a case of thoughts and emotions both influencing one another. In a conversation I had with her as part of the Mindful in May campaign, she explained:

> Our thoughts help shape what emotion we'll feel, but then what emotion we feel shapes the thoughts. So it's not one direction or the other. It's both – and I think we can get pretty side-tracked trying to figure out which comes first. But in practical terms, I think the one that we can have best leverage over is our thoughts. That doesn't mean that the arrow doesn't also go in the other direction.

Our thoughts and emotions are constantly changing from moment to moment, and at a fundamental level, our lives are driven by an attempt to move towards the things that make us feel good and away from what makes us feel bad. This universal behaviour is deeply wired into our biology. In the past this was an advantage that helped keep us away from danger. However, this primitive wiring lacks the sophistication needed to help us navigate our way through the demands of our modern world.

Whereas in ancient times, the nice feeling associated with eating sweet food like berries or fruit helped us find calories that were essential for our survival, these days our desire for sugar often leads us to processed foods. Unlike our ancestors, who may have occasionally come upon berries, we are surrounded by shops and advertising that tempt us to more regularly seek out sugar. Our inner programming, which originally helped us survive by foraging for food, is now leading us to self-destruct with a dangerous overconsumption of sugar. In this case, we must learn how to harness our more sophisticated and evolved prefrontal cortex so we can resist the urges driving us towards the 'pleasant', especially when this is harmful. Our automatic reflex responses need to be more consciously considered to ensure we are moving towards what helps us thrive, rather than what destroys us.

If we are constantly reacting to our ever-changing emotions, either by chasing mindlessly after what feels good or, in contrast, avoiding anything that makes us feel uncomfortable, our lives become very unstable and chaotic. Whether in the workplace or in our personal lives and long-term relationships, we need to be able to stay with emotions that make us feel uncomfortable. This doesn't mean we stay in unpleasant situations that are harming us, such as an abusive relationship with a boss or partner. Rather it's about training ourselves to stay with the difficult feelings as they arise (which can happen so often in our day-to-day lives), and exploring them with curiosity, clarity and self-compassion.

If we can do this, we often discover that, as American writer and mythologist Joseph Campbell explained, 'The cave you fear to enter holds the treasure you seek.' As we turn our attention inward and explore difficult emotions with awareness, we discover that they are often the doorway to our personal growth, awakening and deeper happiness.

Pema Chödrön, a renowned Buddhist teacher, explains that meditation, the practice of learning to stay present to our experience especially when it's uncomfortable, is really about 'helping our nervous systems recalibrate and get more tolerant of unpleasantness in service of greater freedom in our lives'. In this way, meditation builds what she calls 'discomfort resilience'.

Mindfulness helps us ride the waves of our emotions and find the calm within the storm, enabling equanimity and emotional balance.

Managing our emotions is a skill that we are able to learn from a very early age, and the degree to which we actually do learn it often depends on the degree to which our parents could manage their own emotions. For some of us, this important skill of emotional regulation comes later in life, as we realise that our lack of emotional management is having a destructive effect on our careers and personal lives.

Emotions are such a large part of our experience of being human, and the way we navigate them has a profound effect on our happiness. This week as we turn our attention to the domain of thoughts and emotions, we will be developing our self-awareness and emotional intelligence, which is the capacity to recognise how we are feeling at any given moment and then to manage our emotions more effectively. This is a crucial aspect of both our fulfilment and happiness in life, and also a strong predictor of our future success in the world.

The guided mindfulness of thought meditation, which you'll be practising each day this week, is a more advanced practice than the previous ones. It directs our attention to the thought stream and supports us in getting more familiar with the way the mind works, offering a new way of understanding and relating to thoughts and emotions. As Aristotle claimed, 'It is the mark of an educated mind to be able to entertain a thought without accepting it.' As you continue to practise the mindfulness of thought meditation, you will discover that you don't need to believe all of the thoughts that come into your mind. This is a liberating discovery, and one that leads us further along the road to finding greater happiness in our lives.

Day One

MINDFULNESS OF THOUGHT

'The mind is its own place, and in itself can make a heaven of hell, a hell of heaven.'
John Milton

I'm often reminded of the nature of thoughts when playing with my young daughter. Like most toddlers she loves chasing bubbles and squeals with delight as she tries to catch them. As she reaches for them, they pop, vanishing back into the space from which they appeared.

We can think of our thoughts as bubbles – transient entities that appear and disappear in the space of the mind. But we don't always allow our thoughts to just float past – instead we get fixated on them, allowing them undue influence on our behaviour.

We can easily become absorbed by the story of our thoughts, and lose touch with the fact that they are only representations of reality. In an interview with Joseph Goldstein he shares a helpful metaphor to highlight this point:

I often use the example of when we go to the movies, and we get totally engrossed in the story. It can be very compelling. The story and the movie can elicit all kinds of emotions in us. Then the movie is over, and you realise, 'Oh, that was just a movie. Nothing was really happening.' That's the experience we have every time we wake up from being lost in a thought. When we recognise, 'Oh, thinking is present,' we're mindful of it, rather than lost in it.

A regular mindfulness practice helps us recognise our thoughts simply as thoughts, and avoid falling into the unhelpful stories that the mind creates which increase our suffering. We are reminded that while thoughts are real, they are not always true.

This concept is perhaps best highlighted through a story.

I was on my way to a beach holiday, and as I walked towards my seat on the plane, my partner nudged me and whispered that one of Australia's best female surfing champions was in the seat next to mine. I had no idea who she was, but he was excited. As the plane took off, I sensed her body stiffening and noticed out of the corner of my eye that her hands were clasped tightly to the arm rest. She was terrified. I was surprised to see someone who spent her career riding massive waves holding on for dear life as if the plane was about to crash.

As the plane levelled into cruising and her body relaxed, my curiosity around this paradox compelled me into a conversation.

'Are you going on holiday?' I asked.

'Kind of, I'm actually going to compete in a surfing competition,' she replied.

'Have you had any close calls with sharks over your years of surfing?'

'Oh, yes. It's just part of the sport. I see it as us being visitors to their environment, so you just know that there's always a risk. I've had a few times where I'm paddling into a wave and see a massive shark as if it's staring at me through a wall of glass. There've definitely been some close calls where you lose your breath for a moment or two. But surfing is my passion.'

'But you don't like flying much?'

She laughed. 'No, I hate flying. I'm terrified of flying.'

'How is it that you can surf with sharks, but taking off in an aeroplane makes you so scared?'

'I know it doesn't really make sense, but I can't help it. When that plane takes off, my mind spins into a panic with thoughts that tell me the plane is about to crash and I feel terrified.'

Our minds certainly play mysterious tricks on us, and have a profound capacity to sculpt our realities in both good ways and bad. However, in our daily lives this mental trickery can be a lot more subtle and devious. Many of the thoughts that pass through our heads appear so quickly and unconsciously that we are not even aware of their impact on our sense of reality.

Thinking is not the problem in itself. It's how we get hooked by our thoughts and believe them to be true that creates so much extra suffering. It's like having a tiny piece of glass in our foot that we can't see with our naked eye, yet it's there, causing us discomfort. It's only when we shine a bright light on the foot that we see the source of our pain. Mindfulness shines a light on our thoughts, helping us see how they are often a source of extra suffering.

As mentioned in Week One, the continuous flow of thoughts through our mind is an involuntary process. And although thoughts aren't always true, they can shape our experience and in turn our life. As Gandhi famously stated:

Your beliefs become your thoughts,
Your thoughts become your words,
Your words become your actions,
Your actions become your habits,
Your habits become your values,
Your values become your destiny.

There are thoughts we might believe to be true that have been conditioned by our past experiences. These thoughts might include what we perceive as threatening to our safety, who we think we are, what we think we are entitled to and what we believe we have the capacity to do in the world.

As we become more mindful of our thoughts, they become less powerful, and we discover they are not as solid and true as we previously believed. This discovery opens up new possibilities as we are released from the prison of old, limiting thought patterns that may have been holding us back for decades.

FINDING FREEDOM IN PRISON

Fleet Maull is not your average meditation teacher. Although he studied meditation in his early twenties, he was soon swept up in the 1960s drugs, sex and rock'n'roll American counter-culture, which ultimately led him into trouble. In an interview for Mindful in May he shared his experiences:

'I became very alienated and radicalised. I ended up justifying in my own head that it was okay to live outside the system, and I got involved in small-scale drug smuggling. I knew I had to get out of that, but before I could unwind it all, I ended up in federal prison.'

Fleet, a father of one son at the time, was sentenced to thirty years in prison at age thirty-five and served fourteen years. He reflected on his time in prison:

'When I got there, I was absolutely devastated about what I'd done to my family, and my meditation teacher, and especially my son, who was nine years old at the time and was now going to grow up without a dad. For the first time, I stopped compartmentalising my life. I'd been a serious meditation practitioner before going to prison, but that was one part of me, and then I had this other part over here where the tension was, which I self-medicated. All that stopped, and I really dedicated my time in prison to intensive practice and to service.'

While in prison, Fleet taught meditation to fellow inmates and also set up the world's first hospice program within the prison. He explained that being confronted with one's own mortality, and committing to others was probably one of the most transformative things about his journey.

Many people starting out in meditation feel that they need to retreat to a quiet calm place in order to learn how to meditate. However, Fleet's story highlights that no matter what our current reality is, that is where we can begin.

'It's easy in our regular lives to get things working our way. We get our little home set up our way – or our job. We can't protect it completely, but a lot of the time we're able to control our little space. Within that, there's not a lot of feedback. In prison you have no space you can control. It's constant feedback. It was a very auspicious and advantageous place to practise meditation.'

The real path to greater freedom and happiness is through developing enough self-awareness to see the inner chains that keep us hostage. Many of us are living in our own self-created prisons, held back by the beliefs and thoughts that we've mistaken for facts, and that obstruct us from reaching our fullest potential. As Fleet said, 'In many ways we're all doing time, and before you can get free, first you have to see the bars of the prison you've created with your own mind.'

Practise the thought meditation every day this week, and once you become familiar with the practice, I encourage you to stop using the audio guidance and practise in silence. Set a time for yourself – whether five minutes, ten or more – and simply observe your thoughts. You can find the guided meditation at **www.mindlifeproject.com/book**.

This is a more advanced practice, so even if it feels confusing, just be patient and continue to practise without judgement for each day this week.

MINDFULNESS OF THOUGHT GUIDANCE

Purpose

- To mindfully observe thoughts as they come and go.
- To become more familiar with the nature of the mind and develop understanding and recognition of emotions.
- To develop the ability to observe thoughts without engaging with them.
- To discover habitual thought patterns and consider their impact on your broader life.

The practice

- Whether you use the audio guidance or prefer to self-guide, ensure you find a comfortable and quiet place where you won't be disturbed.
- This practice can be done sitting on a chair or cushion or lying down in a comfortable place.
- If you are following the audio meditation, allow it to guide you. If you are self-guiding, set a time for five minutes and close your eyes. Now observe your thoughts as if you were watching bubbles appearing and disappearing in the space of your mind.
- After the practice, consider writing down your thoughts.

Tips

- If you are planning to write your thoughts down at the end of the meditation, try to remember how they link from one to another and use that as a guide.
- If you have trouble locating thoughts, it might help to intentionally bring one to mind – it could be as simple as 'this is a thought' – or bring to mind the image of an object (e.g. a banana). Now keep your attention on the space of the mind where the thoughts or images appear.
- Bring a curiosity to the nature of thoughts: are your thoughts images, sounds, words?
- Notice if you get pulled into the story of a thought, as if pulled into a movie in your mind.

You can listen to the mindfulness of thought meditation by visiting www.mindlifeproject.com/book

An edited transcript of the practice is included below if you'd like more specific instructions before you guide yourself through the practice.

Mindfulness of thought meditation guidance

1. Gently closing your eyes, take a moment to check in with how you're feeling right now. Allow yourself to let go of any concerns about the past or future for a short while. Become aware of the feeling of the body, noticing the areas of contact that the body makes with the chair or the ground.

2. Take a deep breath in and gently let it go. Allow the breath to flow in and out in its natural rhythm, not trying to control it or change it in any way.

3. Rest your attention on the breath as it flows in and out, from moment to moment. Not thinking about the breath but rather feeling the breath, wherever it arises in the body.

4. Shift your attention now from the sensations of the breath to the experience of sounds and hearing. Direct your attention to any sounds that are present within your field of awareness. If at any moment there are no particular sounds to be heard, just notice the silence.

5. When you notice your attention has been carried away by thoughts, simply unhook from these thoughts, letting them go and gently bringing attention back to the sounds that come and go from moment to moment.

6. Now, when you're ready, gently shift your attention from the experience of sounds to the stream of thinking itself. Sounds will continue to come and go, but now direct the focus of attention to thoughts, as they appear and disappear in the space of the mind.

7. If this is a new practice, it can be helpful to deliberately bring to mind a thought, such as 'This is the mind'. Direct your full attention to the thought, this mental event, and when the thought has dissolved back into the space of the mind, keep your attention fixed at this place and watch as the next thought arrives.

8. Just rest your attention on the space of the mind, and notice as thoughts come and go.

9. Pay attention to thoughts as they arise, not as truths or facts, but simply as mental events.

10. Notice the nature of thoughts, their form and content. Maybe they are images or words, or in the form of an internal voice.

11. Notice whether the thoughts have any feelings or emotions attached to them – whether they are pleasant, unpleasant or perhaps neutral.

12. See if you can observe the thoughts as if you were standing behind a waterfall, watching the stream of thoughts pass by like the flowing water.

13. When you realise your attention has been hijacked by thoughts, gently let go of the story or thoughts that had pulled you in, and once again observe the stream of thoughts as they come, hang around and eventually dissolve, without getting caught up or kidnapped by them.

14. Just as the eyes see, the nose smells, the mouth tastes, the mind thinks.

15. Now, in the final moments of this meditation, bring your attention back to the sensations of the breath. Feel the movement of the body as the breath moves in and out. And remember that at any time in the day, you can tune in to your breath, sounds and thought streams as a way of bringing mindfulness to the present moment.

TODAY'S PRACTICE
Watch Your Thoughts

Beyond the guided daily ten-minute meditation, you may like to try watching your thoughts at other times during the day. It's as simple as setting a timer, closing your eyes and watching your thoughts as though you were watching a movie.

During this kind of meditation it's important that you don't try to change your thoughts, push them away or engage with them. Just let them appear and disappear without getting pulled into their stories.

Through regularly observing the mind in this way, you'll start to notice when you've become lost in thinking and become better at unhooking from unhelpful thoughts and bringing yourself back to the moment. You may also start to recognise that you can't fully control what thoughts come into your mind. Just as your heart beats and your breath flows in and out, your mind thinks.

In today's meditation you may have found that when you go looking for thoughts they seem to disappear, whereas when you want your mind to stay in one place – such as on the breath, body sensations or sounds – thoughts seem to constantly pull at your attention.

Sometimes thoughts seem to flow into the mind in a constant stream, and at other times you can notice that there is a gap between your thoughts.

Thoughts may come and go, but between thoughts there is a space, this space is always present and unchanging. This is the space of awareness.

METAPHORS FOR THE MIND

Here are two helpful ways of thinking about the mind:

The mind is like a stage

The stage is like our awareness – a constant, unchanging space from which all thoughts arise. The thoughts are likened to actors that enter and leave the stage. When meditating on thoughts, we simply witness the 'actors' coming and going on the stage of our own mind. In this way we learn how to maintain this observer position, even in the midst of difficult thoughts or emotions.

The mind is like the sky

Just as clouds come and go and can obscure a clear sky, so too do thoughts come and go – and they can obscure the clarity of this unchanging awareness. The sky is boundless, clear and infinite, like our awareness.

Try to find the patterns

As you regularly practise this mindfulness of thought meditation, you'll increasingly notice the thought patterns that drive so much of your life. It may lead you to uncover aspects of yourself that you don't really like: perhaps greed, judgment or fear-based thinking. It's important to bring a kindness and compassion to yourself as you expose these previously hidden imperfections. It also helps to be able to laugh at yourself on occasion.

One such revelation came to me on a silent meditation retreat. The chef on this retreat was the exceptional Sun Hyland (whose recipes are featured in this book), and as a foodie I was looking forward to being nourished. During the first few days of meditation, I noticed my mind spending much of the time contemplating what might be next on the menu. This obsession with meals was no doubt a combination of self-comfort (to get through the boredom of meditating for hours), and an expression of craving. On the first day or two of the retreat, I was always at the front of the lunch line.

After a couple of days of meditating, I gradually started to settle into the process. The meditation was doing its work in helping to slow down the cascade of thoughts, and I was able to gain greater clarity and insight into my habitual reactions. With more space between the thoughts, I was able to watch my unconscious inner programming play out through the day.

Then one day, as the bell rang to signal that lunch was being served, I watched myself jump up and walk briskly towards the lunch hall. Suddenly self-aware, I laughed as I realised there really was no need to rush. The food was abundant and there was plenty of time. I recognised the driving energy that was so familiar in my daily life and realised that I didn't need to hurry in this context. Waiting in line for lunch was not a problem, or an annoyance.

Creating space for ourselves through meditation allows us to recognise the patterns of thinking that drive our behaviour without our conscious awareness. Of course so many of us are struggling to get more done in a day than is humanly possible, but with increased awareness we can see our patterns more clearly and recognise how they are creating a sense of pressure in our lives. This is an important ingredient in developing greater happiness and contentment.

Day Two

MINDFUL EMOTIONS

'The only real voyage of discovery consists not in seeking new landscapes but in having new eyes.'
Marcel Proust

How did you go with the mindfulness of thought practice yesterday?

Another helpful metaphor when doing the mindfulness of thought meditation is to imagine that your thoughts are like trains passing through the station of your awareness. Just as you could stand on a railway platform watching trains continuously arrive and depart, you can also observe your thoughts as they move in and out of your awareness. Every time you realise you've 'gotten on the train' and been carried off by it, simply let the thoughts go and return to observing them as they pass through your mind.

As you continue to practise the mindfulness of thought meditation this week, you'll start to become aware of the relationship between thoughts and emotions. Some thoughts are easy to let go of, but others seem to be more 'sticky'. These thoughts are often associated with an emotion. If during your meditation an emotion becomes quite strong, you can shift your attention from thoughts to the emotion itself, exploring it with curiosity and kindness. Tomorrow we'll investigate the steps to working mindfully with difficult emotions, while in meditation and in life more generally.

Although we prefer to feel emotions such as happiness, difficult emotions are a part of being human. We can't get rid of them, but we can learn how to manage them more constructively.

Difficult emotions such as fear, anger or sadness are often important signals alerting us to the fact that something is going on internally. If we try to supress, avoid or ignore this side of our emotional life, we're denying a part of ourselves, and that can often be the cause of more serious mental health issues such as anxiety or depression. Rather than suppressing or avoiding our emotions, mindfulness asks us to recognise and be curious about them. As bestselling author and researcher Brené Brown says:

'You can't numb those hard feelings without numbing all of our emotions. You cannot selectively numb emotion. So when we numb those hard feelings, we numb joy, we numb gratitude, we numb happiness.'

Paul Ekman, psychologist and emotion guru, discovered seven universal basic emotions experienced by people in all cultures: anger, disgust, contempt, fear, happiness, sadness, surprise. According to Ekman's research, the process of feeling an emotion follows a predictable timeline. It begins with a trigger from the external or internal world, which happens in the context of your current situation and your beliefs. This trigger leads to an emotional experience that is both a feeling and a collection of physical sensations, which then ends with a response – the emotion. Although sometimes the responses we have to our emotions feel automatic and out of our control, we do have a choice in how we respond. The key is being able to sense the 'spark' of emotion – or the impulse – before it leads to an action. Unfortunately, when we're in the grip of an emotion our rational mind goes offline, which makes it hard for us to respond wisely.

Mindfulness can help increase the gap between the impulse and action (or actual acting out of our emotions) so that we can pause and reflect rather than react impulsively. As such, we become aware of the spark of an emotion before it turns into a flame and are able to respond more wisely.

TODAY'S PRACTICE
Laugh It Out

Paul Ekman writes that each of the seven universal emotions activates its own specific group of facial muscles. Even more interestingly, he notes that it's possible to experience an emotion by first activating the facial muscles involved in that particular emotion. Today I invite you to experiment with smiling with your whole face and noticing what impact this has on your mood. Does actively smiling make you feel happier?

Laughter can have a similar effect. Next time you catch yourself in a reactive moment, see if you can interrupt the emotional energy by laughing out loud (even if it feels like a forced laugh!). This can effectively disrupt the heaviness of stress. Even if it feels false or forced, just make yourself laugh. Notice how powerful laughter is in shifting the energy of your mood and bringing more lightness and playfulness into your life.

THE BODY–MIND CONNECTION

A group of psychologists in Germany explored how changing one's facial expressions could affect laughter and happiness. They took two groups of people and asked them to watch cartoons and rate how funny they were. The first group were given a pencil to put between their lips that mimicked a frown, and the others put the pencil between their teeth that mimicked a smile. Those who were in the smiling group found the cartoons much funnier than those who were in the frowning group. We know that smiling communicates happiness, but it's powerful to know that we can use our bodies to change our minds and emotions.

What is called for in this moment?

There are times when our emotions are so big and overwhelming that sitting to meditate just seems impossible. In fact, being still in meditation may not be the most effective action to take at those times. When you're hit with a big emotion it can be helpful to take a moment and ask yourself: *what is called for in this moment?* Just taking a mindful pause and reflecting on this question will bring you closer to what you really need – and that may not be meditation. It may be a walk, a run, or taking yourself to the gym to burn off the emotional energy in your body.

More Resources

Try: Laughing yoga with Dr Madan Kataria, www.laughteryoga.org

Read: Paul Ekman's *Emotions Revealed*

Day Three

EMOTIONAL FIRST AID

'To live wisely is to find composure in it all.'
Jack Kornfield

Even after a few years of regular mindfulness practice I noticed that I was still getting emotionally triggered in some situations. I'd expected that regular meditation should somehow eliminate my emotional reactivity.

I was mistaken.

No matter how dedicated you are to mindfulness, it's inevitable that you're going to 'lose it' at times. Emotions are a part of being human. However, mindfulness training will help you become more aware of your emotional reactions, recover more quickly from them and respond with wisdom.

In his book, *The Yes Brain*, psychiatrist and mindfulness expert Daniel Siegel shares a powerful metaphor for how we can gain greater emotional balance and resilience.

He describes the range of our emotional balance and reactivity as living in the blue, green and red zone of emotions. The green zone, is a state we ideally want to be in most of the time. It's a state of emotional balance where even when challenges arise, we can use our more evolved brain – the prefrontal cortex – to come up with effective responses rather than automatic reactions.

The red zone is a state where we're emotionally triggered, and our sympathetic nervous system has stimulated the fight-or-flight response. In this state, we may notice an increased heart rate, the heat of emotion, and more rapid breathing – all signs of being in a hyperaroused state. In this red zone, we're driven by the more primitive brain that leads us to automatically react, often in ways that make the situation worse. We are less resourced.

The blue zone is another state triggered by stress, but it's a hypo-aroused response, triggered by our parasympathetic nervous system, which leads to more of a withdrawal and avoidance of situations. Think of a freeze response or helpless victim state.

The key to our resilience lies in expanding 'the window of our green zone', so that we can meet challenges with less reactivity and more responsiveness. That doesn't mean we'll stop feeling difficult emotions such as fear or anger, but rather that we'll be able to make room for them without being mindlessly driven by them.

Siegel writes, 'Reactivity blocks resilience and receptivity promotes it.' When we are able to pause and bring mindfulness to our emotions, we widen the green zone and have a better ability to respond wisely and maintain greater emotional balance.

Mindfulness really is a crucial foundation for building resilience, and it's the regularity of the practice that's important.

With this in mind, here is a helpful mindfulness practice that supports us in widening the green zone of our emotional state. It was inspired by my time working in emergency departments of the hospital. As doctors we were taught the ABC of physical resuscitation. It was an acronym describing a step-by-step process of immediately checking the airways, breathing and circulation when someone presented in an unconscious state. Having this acronym helped us jump into action without having to think too much about what we needed to do. At the height of an emergency, when my amygdala (page 20) took over and the rational, thinking mind tended to go offline, I was able to move into action without needing my prefrontal cortex to help me solve the problem.

In daily life, when you're emotionally triggered and your prefrontal cortex is hijacked by your amygdala, whether you're feeling anger, fear or agitation, you need a simple reminder to help you work with the emotion mindfully. Based on my emergency response ABC, I created the mindful **ABC of Emotional First Aid**.

A: Acknowledge

- Acknowledge that the emotion is present.
- We can label the emotion as a way of clearly acknowledging that it is present.
- When we get emotionally triggered, it's very easy to get completely consumed by the emotion. We very quickly lose our capacity for observation and curiosity. This step invites us to pause in the midst of an overwhelming emotion and label it, either out loud or by simply noting it silently to ourselves.
- This acknowledgement is the first step in having more freedom to respond wisely in the face of an emotional response.

B: Be open and breathe

- Be open to the emotion that has arrived, allowing it to be present.
- We are wired to pull away from emotions such as anger, sadness or fear; they don't feel good in our bodies. This second step asks you to be open and stay with whatever emotion has been activated, remembering that difficult emotions are a normal part of being human.
- Rather than suppressing or denying our emotions, this step encourages us to make room for them. Interestingly, by being open to whatever emotion is present, we actually allow them to flow through us, rather than linger and get stuck as we expend more energy trying to push them away.
- Use the breath as a way to stay anchored to yourself in the midst of an overwhelming emotion, and use the outbreath to release any tension in the body associated with the emotion. With each outbreath you can silently say to yourself, 'I send compassion to this particular emotion.' This phrase can interrupt the reactivity and help you soothe yourself.

C: Curiously explore

- Curiously explore and turn towards the experience.
- Ask yourself, where do I feel this emotion in my body? What sensations are associated with this emotion? What am I believing?
- The key to this step is to bring a quality of kindness and gentleness to the investigation, as if you were a parent gently exploring what has upset your child.
- Where do you feel the emotion in your body?

- Be curious about the quality of the emotion. Do you experience it as solid and permanent, or do you notice it changes as you pay attention?

D: Don't be hard on yourself and de-identify with the emotion

- This step asks you to use difficult emotions as an opportunity to develop your self-compassion. Remind yourself that, just like every other human on the planet, you are not perfect, and will inevitably be thrown off-centre and react in ways you feel ashamed about.
- It is also an opportunity to remember the universal truth of impermanence, the fact that everything is transient and that emotions are no exception.
- De-identifying from emotion means that you recognise that this emotion is a transient phenomenon, rather than some underlying personal deficit. You can experiment with silently noting to yourself, 'I am noticing the feeling of [name the emotion] …' Or simply, 'Here is anger'. Rather than thinking, 'I'm angry', this subtle shift in perspective through labelling reminds us of the impermanent nature of emotions. In this way we can hold emotions more lightly, and forgive ourselves more easily when we behave in ways that feel reactive or unwise.

When you experience a difficult emotion, you can practise the ABC of Emotional First Aid by simply taking yourself through the steps in your own mind. Otherwise it can be used retrospectively once the emotion has passed, as a way of making sense of the situation and developing an understanding of your personal emotional triggers. I've even found it extremely useful to use the ABC steps as prompts for journaling about difficult emotions. Often when we get emotionally triggered, we perceive one dominant emotion (such as anger), but by pausing and curiously exploring that emotion, we discover that other emotions may be hidden beneath. For example when we are angry, there can be more vulnerable emotions such as disappointment, sadness, hurt or fear hiding beneath the anger. Bringing mindfulness to our emotions gives us more insight and brings us closer to the heart of the matter, supporting wisdom and self-awareness.

TODAY'S PRACTICE
Name it to tame it

Think of the last time you felt anger. Perhaps it was triggered by a work colleague, a boss or someone close to you, such as a partner or child. The emotion often gets triggered when you feel you're not being understood or someone is taking advantage of you. Reflect on the fact that anger gets triggered automatically. You may feel your heart racing or your body temperature rise. Your body may tense up. There is a surge of energy that compels you to act in some way to relieve the tension. This immediate and overwhelming emotional response, which is often out of proportion to the stimulus that triggered it, is what Daniel Goleman, author of *Emotional Intelligence*, calls the '**amygdala hijack**'. In these moments, the amygdala (page 20) hijacks the thinking, rational brain (prefrontal cortex) and sets off a cascade of events that aims to protect us from perceived threat.

No matter how much you meditate, you'll never eliminate anger from your emotional repertoire: it's a normal human emotion. However, you can bring more awareness to your emotions when they get triggered, and in this way reduce their negative impact on your life.

One way of reducing the intensity of an amygdala hijack is to label our emotions when they arise. By labelling the emotion, we activate the prefrontal cortex, which sends inhibitory neurotransmitters to the amygdala, calming down those reactive emotions. In the words of psychiatrist and mindfulness expert Dr Daniel Siegel, when it comes to an emotion, we have to 'name it to tame it'.

As we develop mindfulness, or a capacity to clearly observe what is happening from moment to moment, we can bring this awareness to our emotional world. As we become more mindful of difficult emotions, we reinforce neural pathways that help us remember to pause when we're in the heat of an emotion, and use the most evolved part of the brain, the prefrontal cortex, to calm ourselves down.

MINDFUL PARENTING ABC

Parenting is a rich source of mindfulness training and provides many opportunities to apply mindful emotional first aid. On a good day, it's an exhilarating spiritual journey of epic proportions, where we have the privilege of witnessing our most creative project flourish. On a bad day, it's an exhausting, frustrating ride where we are tested beyond our limits through sleep deprivation, tantrums, mastitis, stress, relationship tension or self-doubt.

Mindfulness has certainly been a crucial part of my parenting survival tool kit, not only in managing the challenges, but also in helping me remember to be present and appreciate the daily magic amidst the domestic monotony.

I've found mindfulness particularly helpful for managing tantrums, so here are a few tips on how to deal with tantrums using the emotional ABC.

Acknowledge

When tantrums strike, it's easy to lose your calm. Your child's cry is designed to set off your emotional alarm so they get your immediate attention and avoid potential threats. However, tantrums are a developmentally normal phenomenon that most often only reflect a child's attempt to assert themselves and develop agency. To help ground yourself and move from stressed to calm when your child is having a tantrum, first consciously recognise what's happening and silently label it 'tantrum'. This is the first step to avoid getting lost in the emotional storm. By actively labelling 'tantrum' you'll be activating the higher regions of your brain that allow you to think more clearly, problem-solve and stay calm rather than panic. Then acknowledge the feelings your child is having and label them. For example, 'I understand you really want to have a biscuit but we need to eat a healthy dinner first.' 'I can see you're really upset.' This helps your child learn about their emotional world.

Be open and breathe

Once you've recognised and labelled what's happening, bring your attention to your breath. You may notice that your breath is becoming restricted or fast as your emotions are triggered. Slow your breath down and extend your exhalation. This will quiet your entire nervous system, keeping you calm rather than reactive, and helping you make better decisions about what is needed. Turn to your breath as a way of staying grounded and not losing your cool.

Curiously explore

Once you've connected with your breath and calmed your own nervous system down, activate your curiosity and ask yourself, 'What is needed in this moment?' If you're in public, it may be picking your child up and leaving the situation. If you're at home, it might simply be anchoring to your own breathing while the tantrum passes, making an empathetic statement to your child, or diverting their attention with distraction. When we are emotionally triggered into a stress response, we lose our capacity to make wise decisions. Mindfulness helps us regain this wisdom and make better decisions, especially when under pressure.

Don't be hard on yourself

When dealing with the many challenges of parenting, self-compassion is a powerful antidote to any feelings of inadequacy that can arise. When tantrums happen, it's easy to get frustrated at your child and at yourself. So when the tantrum has passed, take a moment to remind yourself that this a very normal part of a child's development. Think of all the other parents who may be dealing with a tantrum in this very moment, and connect to this sense of shared humanity. You're not in this alone. Practise active self-compassion by putting your hand on your heart and offering yourself some phrases of warmth, love and reassurance. Silently wish yourself well by repeating, 'I'm doing the best I can.'

Day Four

MINDFULNESS FOR WISER DECISION-MAKING

'When you have to make a choice and don't make it, that is in itself a choice.'
William James

How are you finding the mindfulness of thought practice?

Have you had an opportunity to apply the mindful ABC to a difficult emotion?

Emotions can be triggered by external or internal events. As we've noted, while other people in our lives can trigger it, often it is our inner thought processes that spark the response. One aspect of thinking that can cause us stress and confusion is the process of making difficult decisions.

Many of us get really stuck when faced with making decisions, and mindfulness can be a very helpful tool in supporting us in this kind of challenge. As you become more aware of the body sensations associated with particular emotions, not just the thoughts, you'll find a deeper source of wisdom that is your intuition or 'gut feeling'.

We have spent the last few days learning how to recognise our emotions and not let them automatically dictate our behaviour, but there are times when our emotions can be powerful guides that help us move forward in the face of difficult decisions. So in this way, mindfulness helps us get better at discerning which emotions are driven by fear and lead us away from what we truly want in our lives, and which ones are driven by wisdom guiding us towards what we genuinely desire.

As a recovering perfectionist, making decisions – especially big ones – has never been easy for me, and I have often found myself obsessing over trying to make 'the best' decision.

The word 'decision' comes from the Latin *decidere*, which means 'to cut off'. Decisions lead to change, which inevitably come with losses and gains, and for many of us the thought of closing doors and making the 'wrong' decision can be deeply uncomfortable. We each have our own unique way of making decisions. Some of us dive into taking action in the face of a decision, then become overwhelmed post-decision as the mind starts analysing the situation. Alternatively, some of us end up in analysis paralysis and then finally make a choice once we've exhausted all possible outcomes in our mind.

I fall into the second group. Mindfulness has helped me get better at unhooking from the analysis and connecting with the wisdom that exists in my intuition, so that I can make decisions with greater ease. When I was first considering having a child, I spent so much time gathering information about it that my friends started calling it my 'research PhD'. It was as if I believed that by knowing everything there was to know on the subject, I could come to the 'right' decision, and I would eliminate the inevitable uncertainty that comes with becoming a parent. I discovered a hidden fear of the unknown that was prolonging my research and obstructing me from making a decision.

Mindfulness training has been crucial in helping me tune in to my feelings and intuition to solve a dilemma, rather than getting caught in analytical mind loops.

Although philosophers over the centuries warned that we should always turn to reason over emotion, science has revealed that our emotions are actually useful signals that can help to support our decisions. In his book *Descartes' Error*, neuroscientist Antonio Damasio describes a patient whose inability to experience emotions had a devastating effect on his decision-making and his life. Elliot was a successful lawyer who underwent surgery for a brain tumour, which led to an injury in his prefrontal cortex – a part that we know is crucial for receiving messages and signals from the emotional brain centre. After the surgery, his intelligence was unaffected – he could think, speak and do all of the things he could do before. However, his life fell apart through poor decision-making. His family explained that simple decisions such as what to eat or how to file his work papers would absorb him for hours.

Damasio tested Elliot's brain and found that while his thinking and reasoning were unaffected by the surgery, when asked what date he would like to come back for another check-up, Elliot could give a list of things that were coming up but was unable to make a decision. Damasio's theory was that when we are faced with decisions, we unconsciously receive body signals associated with different emotions that help us filter one outcome from the next. Without access to his emotions and 'body wisdom', Elliot could not weigh up what mattered most to him.

In fact, the term 'trust your gut' has a scientific basis, thanks to a part of the brain called the 'basal ganglia'. According to Daniel Goleman, our basal ganglia stores information about everything we do and keeps track of our decisions, like a database that remembers everything from our lives. It isn't connected to our verbal brain and so it can't communicate with our reason, but it is connected to the gut and may therefore play an important role in what we call 'intuition', our non-verbal feeling system. It can't tell us what it knows in words, so it tells us what it knows through the body, through our feelings.

TODAY'S PRACTICE
Write from your gut

As much as I value science and evidence, I am fascinated by all the aspects of the world that we believe exist but that we can't yet measure or prove. One of these areas is the body's 'distributed intelligence'.

In his book *Memories, Dreams, Reflections*, Carl Jung describes visiting Taos, New Mexico, to learn about Native American culture. He spoke with an elder named Mountain Lake, who expressed to Jung that white people always seemed uneasy and restless: 'We do not understand them. We think that they are mad.'

Jung asked him why he thought white people were mad.

'They say they think with their heads,' Mountain Lake explained. 'We think here.' He pointed to his heart.

In the Western world, we too easily dismiss the body as no more than a mode of transportation for our heads, rather than an additional source of intelligence. Our language is a powerful reflection of the way we perceive reality, and in English (and most other Western languages), we define ourselves with two separate words – we are a 'mind' and a 'body'. In contrast, the single Japanese word '*kokoro*' translates to 'heart–mind–spirit', which reflects an understanding that these parts are not entirely separate, but are really one integrated whole, which is a more accurate reflection of the reality.

Is there a decision that you're avoiding because it feels too hard to make? This might be a good time to try accessing your intuition.

This mindful writing exercise invites you to bring your awareness back into the body

1. Take ten minutes to settle yourself by choosing one of the guided meditations from this book.
2. After the practice is finished, bring your awareness into the region of your gut.
3. Notice any bodily sensations in this area.
4. Now set a timer for five minutes and write as if you were the gut writing to 'yourself'.
5. Ask your gut to tell you what you need to pay attention to at the moment.
6. If your mind starts to get judgmental or agitated, just imagine you are unscrewing your head and putting it next to you for five minutes.
7. Allow the pen to flow.
8. You may need to keep remembering to come back to resting your awareness on the belly.

In terms of managing a decision with greater ease, here are a few more steps that can help you to gain a different perspective on the dilemma:

Clearly label the decision that you're grappling with

Sometimes we get caught in thought loops about decisions that really aren't that important. Other times, we're faced with decisions that have no positive outcome as an option. Recognising and labelling what type of decision we're facing provides a broader perspective on it. This brings attention to what is really going on so we can gain deeper insight into what is occurring beneath the surface of our busy minds.

Ask yourself what this is really about

Often a decision may seem like it's about one thing, but through further investigation, you'll discover it's about something deeper and more universal, like the fear of the unknown or a need to be in control. When I catch myself clinging to the need for a perfect decision, I remind myself that there is no way of absolutely knowing its consequences. Instead of letting myself be trapped by the need for certainty, I turn my mind to a challenge that I have faced and managed, and I tap into my inner resource of resilience. I remind myself that I'm making the best decision I can, knowing all that I know, and that I will have the strength and resilience to manage its outcomes.

Be aware of what the mind is doing in relation to the decision

If you are just obsessively replaying thoughts through your mind, recognise this as anxious thinking. Let the thoughts go and bring your attention back to the breath as a way of unhooking from it.

Make sure you have all the information you need to make the decision

Are there missing bits of information that might help you make your decision? Contact anyone you think may be helpful in giving you the information you need to take a step forward.

Reflect on your values and let them drive your decision

For example, if one of your values is courage, recognise that perhaps the thing obstructing your decision-making process is fear, and reassure yourself that just as you've managed difficulties in the past, you have the resilience to manage any of the outcomes. If one of your values is authenticity and honesty, then you can allow this value to drive the decision to have that difficult conversation you've been avoiding.

Be compassionate with yourself

Big decisions often take longer to make than we'd like. This can cause frustration and create a feeling of 'stuckness' in our lives that can easily turn into self-criticism. Remember to actively maintain self-compassion as you navigate the complexity of your decision. Remind yourself that sometimes answers don't come according to the timelines we have in our mind.

Some questions for your reflection

- How do you make big decisions or small decisions?
- What have you learned about how you make decisions?
- What gets in the way of you making a decision?
- What have you learned about the wisdom of the mind, heart and gut through making decisions?
- What wisdom can you call upon from lessons you've learned through previous decisions that can support you in any current decisions you need to make?

Day Five

MINDFUL COMMUNICATION
AND RELATIONSHIPS

'Listening is a magnetic and strange thing, a creative force. The friends who listen to us are the ones we move toward. When we are listened to, it creates us, makes us unfold and expand.'

Karl Menninger

As is often the case in medical training, we were often encouraged to use ourselves as research subjects. One day, while learning about the organs of the body, my class was asked to gently scrape our own tongues and put the sample under our microscope to see the pattern of cells. Incredibly, the tongue scraping was like a purple and pink Indigenous dot painting, with intricate patterns and circular cell shapes organised in distinct clusters. I zoomed in further and magnified a taste bud, revealing details of each of the hundreds of cells in this biological artistic masterpiece.

Just as our physical bodies are a complex matrix of cells that interconnect to create organs and systems, from the moment of our birth we are connected to a web of other individuals who not only support us, but literally shape our brains and our destinies.

Although we each commonly think of ourselves as an 'I', we are wired to be 'we's, and our brains are wired for connection. As soon as we come into the world, our social interactions are being translated into the physical architecture of our bodies. As Louis Cozolino writes in *The Neuroscience of Human Relationships*,

> There are no single human brains – brains only exist within networks of other brains. Without mutually stimulating interactions, people and neurons wither and die. In neurons this process is called apoptosis; in humans it is called depression, grief and suicide. Relationships are our natural habitat.

This makes sense of the research suggesting that loneliness is more dangerous for our health than smoking, and a significant risk factor for conditions ranging from cardiovascular disease to Alzheimer's. In order to flourish, we need to feel connected. Research into three of the world's longest-living communities (including Sardinians in Italy, Okinawans in Japan, and a community in Loma Linda, California) has revealed that for these individuals, 'staying socially connected' was one of the secrets to their longevity.

For centuries, enforced solitude has been used as one of the cruellest forms of punishment. Mohamed Barud Ali, a Somalian humanitarian and political activist, was sentenced to lifetime solitary confinement after a minor act that the Somalian government considered treasonous. It was 1981, and Somalia was in the grip of a military dictatorship. Mohamed had been married just three months before being arrested.

He shared details of his confinement with journalist Gregory

Warner on the podcast *Rough Translation*. 'It was strictly forbidden to talk to your neighbours. So you'd walk forward and backward pacing up and down a cell that was two metres by two metres. I was frightened of going to a certain area in my mind where I would commit suicide without knowing, or wanting to.'

One day, two years into his sentence, he heard a whisper from the neighbouring cell: 'Learn the ABC.' This whisper was followed by some quiet knocking on the wall. The inmate in the neighbouring cell was Dr Adan Abokor, a medical doctor and friend from Mohamed's life before prison. Abokor had ingeniously created a type of Morse code and was communicating to Mohamed through the walls. Abokor was taken out of the cell after two years of confinement to be given a new set of clothes, and during this transient break in his punishment he was unexpectedly allowed to take one of the many books he'd brought to prison back to his cell. He chose *Anna Karenina* by Tolstoy, because it was the longest of all of his books.

Over the next several months Abokor read the eight hundred-page book to Mohamed using Morse code. The story was tapped through the wall and communicated through the walls to the other eight inmates also in solitary confinement. In this way, for six years, the men kept each other company.

Mohamed recounts: 'We used to tell jokes through the walls. One guy would say, "What are you all laughing about?" and the joke would travel through the walls so everyone could enjoy it. The guards just thought our laughing was a sign of our collective insanity from our years in confinement.' The need to connect overcame these seemingly impossible circumstances.

One of the longest-running studies of human development, called the Grant study, looked at a group of 268 male students from Harvard and followed their lives to explore what factors were most important in determining happiness. It is the longest study of its kind and gives us some valuable insight into what contributes to a flourishing life. The director of the study shared that 'the clearest message we get from this 75-year study is this: good relationships keep us happier and healthier'. Mindfulness can support us in deepening the connections and relationships in our lives through improving how we communicate.

TODAY'S PRACTICE
Mindful Conversation

Conversations are a great opportunity to practise being mindful – and mindfulness in turn supports us in experiencing intimacy. Our lives run at such a hectic speed, with competing forces pulling our attention in all directions, that bringing our full attention to someone is truly rare. By being mindful in our conversations, we can develop empathy as well as insight into and understanding of the perspective of those we interact with. It's a challenging practice, but one that can deepen and enrich both our personal and professional relationships.

Experiment today with these twelve steps to having a mindful C.O.N.V.E.R.S.A.T.I.O.N.

C: Clear intention to be mindful

Set a clear intention about how you are going to use your attention in this conversation. Recognise that you are going to make an extra effort to be fully present.

O: Open to the other person

Often during conversations we can be caught up in our own concerns and thoughts. When we mindfully communicate, we consciously open our awareness to include a sense of our own body and emotional state, while also making space to be open to the other person.

N: Non-verbal communication

Pay attention to the person's non-verbal communication: their posture, eye contact, and facial expressions. A large part of communication is transmitted through our non-verbal gestures and signs.

V: Voice quality and content

Notice the pitch, volume, pauses and the energy in the other person's speech. Pay attention to whether the content of their words is congruous with the way in which they are saying them. For example, someone may tell you they are really happy, but their voice tone may communicate the opposite.

E: Engage with a beginner's mind

Remember to bring a beginner's mind to the conversation. Activate your curiosity and allow yourself to be surprised by the other person. Drop any assumptions you may have about the other person or how a conversation is going to unfold.

R: Resist interrupting

When we are in conversation it can be easy to fall into habitual ways of communicating. Some of us have a habit of talking too much and not allowing enough space for the other person to express themselves. For others it may be a habit of listening and not sharing our thoughts, because of shyness or a belief that what we have to say isn't valuable. A common conversational habit is the tendency to interrupt, reflecting our general lack of patience. We can bring more awareness to the way we communicate by noticing our urge to speak, and at that moment taking a breath and reflecting on whether this is interrupting the other person.

S: Speak the truth

Sometimes we don't speak the truth because we want to avoid conflict, or we don't want to be disliked by others. Be aware of what you are saying and stay connected to what is true for you.

A: Allow pauses

Many of us are uncomfortable with silence and so we speak to fill the space. Notice if you have a tendency to fill the space and don't be afraid to pause in conversations.

T: Tune in to your body

When in conversation, it can be easy to lose touch with your own feelings. In mindful conversations, you're invited to be present to the other person's non-verbal signs and also maintain some awareness of your own feelings and body sensations. This can be particularly helpful in difficult conversations where you might be emotionally triggered. By staying aware of your own emotional state, you can respond more effectively to others, especially when you're under pressure.

I: Invite a non-judgmental attitude

Our minds have a tendency to constantly judge others. This judging mind stems from our ancient survival instincts: we are constantly scanning for danger in our environment. However, we can be quick to judge others in conversation, and this closes our capacity to really see the person as they are.

O: Observe your mind's tendency to drift

During mindful conversations, we are using the other person as the object of our meditation. Just as our attention wanders during meditation, when you notice your mind has drifted away from the conversation, gently bring your attention back to the words or physical presence of the other person.

N: Notice when you feel emotionally triggered

Conversations are a complex exchange between people, and without realising it, we can be emotionally triggered by people's words or responses. Pay particular attention to the feeling of being triggered while in conversation with others. By maintaining a sense of your emotional state throughout conversations, you are better resourced to respond wisely to challenging interactions.

MINDFUL DIALOGUE

You can formalise this idea a little more by arranging a 'mindful dialogue' with a friend, relative or partner. Unlike the mindful conversation, which only requires one person to be practising, the mindful dialogue requires both people to be practising.

Here is a guide to the mindful dialogue

1. Find a good time when no one is rushing.
2. Ask your friend or partner if you can have a mindful dialogue.
3. Decide who is talking and who is listening.
4. Set a timer for five minutes. The listener opens with a question: 'What would you like to talk about?'
5. The speaker has five minutes to talk freely about anything they like.
6. The listener's role is to be completely mindful, without talking or responding with thoughts or advice, to what is being said.
7. The listener then takes three minutes to reflect back what was heard, without overlaying opinion or advice.
8. The speaker then takes a minute to reflect back what it felt like to be listened to.
9. Swap roles and practise again.
10. If you are unsure what to talk about, the listener can make up whatever question they choose.

Some suggested questions to experiment with

- What interests you deeply?
- What makes you feel most alive?
- What is something you used to love doing that you'd enjoy bringing back into your life?
- What in your life, right now, is calling for your attention?
- What would you do if you had more courage?
- What is something you appreciate most in your life?
- What gives your life most meaning?

Day Six

MINDFUL SELF-INQUIRY

'If you want the truth, I'll tell you the truth: Listen to the secret sound,
the real sound, which is inside you.'
Kabir

As the quality of our attention becomes more focused and clear, we can explore the practice of mindful self-inquiry. This is a way to access deeper wisdom by turning our focused attention to a question. David Whyte, the English poet, describes 'a beautiful question' as one that has the power to shift our thinking, catalyse inner change and open us to new possibilities aligned with our deepest longings and truth. As Whyte explains:

The ability to ask beautiful questions, often in very unbeautiful moments, is one of the great disciplines of a human life. And a beautiful question starts to shape your identity as much by asking it as it does by having it answered. You just have to keep asking.

And before you know it, you will find yourself actually shaping a different life, meeting different people, finding conversations that are leading you in those directions that you wouldn't even have seen before.

The conversations we have with ourselves – both conscious and unconscious – are the foundations of our future. By asking ourselves 'beautiful questions' we can begin new inner conversations, expanding what is possible and aligning more deeply with our purpose in the world.

TODAY'S PRACTICE
Six Steps for Practising the Mindful Inquiry

In today's exercise, we contemplate a question or theme with curiosity, openness and presence. The wisdom that emerges from the heart can be quite surprising.

1. Sit in meditation using this week's guided practice to help settle your mind and bring you into deeper clarity and presence.
2. When you have finished your meditation, bring to mind a question, word or theme you'd like to investigate (you can either use the suggested themes below, or anything else you would like to explore more deeply).
3. Silently repeat the question or word to yourself a few times. Rest your attention on the area of your heart, noticing any sensations that are present.
4. Don't seek out answers, but rather allow them to arrive as naturally as the inbreath, without effort. Trust the

wisdom of your own heart to bring answers and new insights to the foreground of your awareness. Sit in silence for five minutes and see what emerges. Be patient, and if nothing comes to you, stay with the question or word a little longer.

5. Get some paper and a pen, and set the timer for five minutes. Write out anything that comes to mind in relation to your question or word. Let the pen flow across the page without stopping or censoring your thoughts. As an experiment, you can also try to use your non-dominant hand, which can often bring surprising discoveries as it activates the other side of your brain.

6. If no clear answers arise, put the question or word to the back of your mind and let it rest there for a few days. Before you go to bed at night, invite your dreams to incorporate the question. Often our dreams can be a powerful source of wisdom and guidance if we actively offer them a question.

There is no right or wrong in the process of mindful self-inquiry, just see what you discover for yourself.

Here are some questions and themes you can explore using mindful self-inquiry

- What could I let go of in order to make things feel easier in my life?
- What could I bring to my relationships to create more connection and love?
- If I had more courage, what would I do?
- What matters most to me?

As well as contemplating questions, you can also focus on a theme and explore the relevance of this theme in your life. You can choose a theme from the list below, then sit for five minutes and contemplate it. Then take a few minutes to journal your reflections on how the theme you have chosen is relevant in your life at the moment.

Some themes to consider

Impermanence: Everything is constantly changing in our lives, yet sometimes we live as if things stay the same and we're surprised by change. From the cycles of our breath, to our thoughts that come and go, or our emotions that come in waves, everything is changing. Sit for ten minutes and contemplate the truth of impermanence in your life.

Patience: Patience is a great virtue. The ability to sit back when we have the urge to lean forward is a powerful practice which allows us to manage times of transition. Sit for ten minutes and contemplate your relationship to patience.

Gratitude: Gratitude is the attitude of noticing the good in our lives and appreciating all that we have from moment to moment. Sit for ten minutes and contemplate your relationship to gratitude.

Contentment: Contentment is the feeling of being completely peaceful in this moment without allowing strong urges, cravings or desires to pull you into the next moment. Sit for ten minutes and contemplate your relationship to contentment.

Day Seven

MANAGING THE COMMON MEDITATION OBSTACLES

'Meditation is a microcosm, a model, a mirror. The skills we practise when we sit are transferable to the rest of our lives.'
Sharon Salzberg

If you're still reading and practising, that is a truly great outcome, and an important step to achieving greater happiness in your life. Even if you're not practising every day, take a moment to consider whether you've been more mindful in daily life than when you began this one-month mindfulness program.

With every new habit we invite into our lives, we inevitably face obstacles and resistance. As you've no doubt discovered, some of the common obstacles that arise during meditation include restlessness, agitation, boredom, anxiety, impatience, sleepiness, doubt and self-criticism (just to name a few). These are often the same challenges or blind spots that arise in our everyday lives.

An essential aspect of being mindful is noticing the way we relate to our experiences. When practising mindfulness, it's helpful to actively remind yourself to bring a friendly, kind and accepting attitude to whatever experience arises in the moment. This doesn't mean you have to like what is happening, just bring an openness and curiosity to whatever is present.

A HINT

Take a moment to check in with yourself and notice if there is any niggling guilt about not having meditated as much as you had intended. With the next outbreath, let go of that guilt. This is an opportunity to get back on board for the remainder of the month.

TODAY'S PRACTICE
Tackle the Five Obstacles

For thousands of years, meditators have struggled with the many obstacles that can disrupt a practice. There are five in particular that commonly intrude along the meditation path. These inner obstacles have been identified in the traditional Buddhist texts as mental energies that obstruct our clarity, happiness and wisdom. It's important to know about them because rather than reading them as signs that we're really bad meditators, we can simply consider them predictable hurdles that are likely to arise along the journey to greater freedom, happiness and growth in our lives. As we learn how to navigate these obstacles in our meditation practice, we discover that we can meet similar challenges in our everyday life with ease and wisdom.

The five obstacles are: desire, aversion, sleepiness, restlessness and doubt.

Desire

Desire is a fascinating force in our lives that can take many different forms. There is the desire that directs us towards our deepest happiness, which might include the wish to become the wisest version of ourself, or to be of service in the world. However, there is another form of desire, which in the ancient meditation texts is referred to as 'craving'. This is the intense feeling of needing something in order to feel satisfied. It may offer us a form of temporary happiness, but ultimately it is the basis of addiction and moves us away from a more enduring happiness.

Craving is that feeling of 'I need this', 'I want this', and it tends to take over the mind, making it fixate obsessively on the object of craving, whether that's food, alcohol, getting a 'like' on Facebook, sex or being materially successful. It's an obstacle to our happiness because it seems to promise satisfaction, yet inevitably leaves us wanting more.

As I sit writing this book at a local cafe, I'm aware of a strong craving for one of the sweet treats in the cabinet behind me. Every few sentences, I turn my head to the cabinet, trying to resist my urge to call the waitress over. Rather than impulsively following this desire, I experiment with bringing mindfulness to it. I ask myself what is going through my mind and discover thoughts such as: 'I want to taste something sweet', 'I really want it', 'This is what I need', 'I'm tired and I need a pick-me-up'.

I bring mindfulness – the open, curious, present-moment awareness – to this feeling of craving in my body and discover a subtle flutter of energy in my chest and a slight ache in my jaw. I notice saliva building in my mouth. It feels really hard to resist this craving, but through mindfulness I shift my attention away from the sweet and towards this uncomfortable feeling of 'wanting'. Even though I know this desire will pass, while in its grip I feel a tug of energy urging me to take action and order the sweet. There's a sense that I will be fulfilled once I get to eat it. But I know that although I'll experience some momentary satisfaction, this will only last until the next craving, and through succumbing to this craving, I will have reinforced the habit of eating sugar, making it a stronger force in my life. When I explore the nature of this urge more deeply, I discover that it's my mind and body seeking something pleasant to shift me out of passing feelings of 'I'm too tired to write' and 'This is really hard'.

If I was happy to be eating sugar, then this craving would not be such a problem. However, I have become a prisoner to this habit, and I want to regain my freedom and return to a healthier diet. In this moment, craving and desire are leading me away from what I truly value: better health and more control over my unhealthy behaviour.

Although you may not be a sweet tooth yourself, I'm pretty confident that in some area of your life, you can relate to the feeling of a craving pulling you away from what you value. Maybe it's a craving to use social media that's getting in the way of your focus at work, or a craving to lie on the couch when you'd intended to exercise.

The point isn't that we need to resist our desires all of the time. Mindfulness simply offers us a way to take the reins back and gain more control over our behaviours, rather than be caught in habits that are in conflict with what we really want for ourselves. It allows us to pause before acting, and consciously discern whether it's a desire we should follow, or one we should let pass.

In this way mindfulness supports freedom in our lives.

SURF YOUR CRAVINGS

Craving is like a wave of energy that builds and then calms. Through focusing our attention on the *feeling* of craving, rather than the *object* of what we crave, mindfulness becomes the surfboard that allows us to ride the wave of craving with awareness, rather than tumble unconsciously into old habits that keep us stuck.

Cravings offer us another opportunity to put the mindful ABC of emotional first aid into practice.

Acknowledge that a craving is present.

Be open and breathe.

Be open to the experience of craving and allow it to be exactly as it is. Avoid trying to push it away.

As you feel the discomfort of an unsatisfied craving, bring your attention to your breath and use the outbreath to release any tension in your body that may be associated with the emotion.

Curiously explore.

Bring curiosity to the physical feeling of craving. Where do you experience craving in your body? What's the quality of the sensations associated with it? Do you feel constricted, agitated or restless?

Stay with the feeling of craving and notice how it naturally rises, peaks and falls over time. Imagine it as a wave in the ocean: building, reaching its peak, and then disappearing back into the calm water.

Through resisting the craving, you can start to break the habit loop and free yourself from automatic behaviours that are obstructing you from your deepest happiness and wellbeing.

Aversion

This is the opposite of desire, and can be expressed as anger or fear. It's the feeling of not wanting something, or an impulse to push it away. Aversion might express itself as irritation with something or someone, and an inability to let it go. This feeling of aversion comes up frequently while we meditate, often showing up as irritation at something we feel is getting in the way of our practice – perhaps a sound or sensation that we find uncomfortable and that we want to stop. Maybe the words or sounds of the meditation guidance irritate us. In life there are endless moments where we feel aversion, whether we're stuck in peak-hour traffic, or faced with a painful physical sensation or difficult work situation. The beauty of learning mindfulness is that aversion becomes an opportunity to practise mindfulness and ultimately transform an obstacle into a potential doorway to greater freedom and happiness.

Anger often arises when we have an expectation of how things are supposed to be. Mindfulness is not about eliminating anger, but rather about being able to recognise that you are in the middle of feeling anger or aversion, and becoming able to pause and just let the emotion pass.

When we are experiencing aversion to something, it can be hard to let go of the feeling of wanting things to be different. We believe that suffering results from the object of our aversion. However, as Joseph Goldstein highlights in his book *Mindfulness*, holding on to anger and aversion is like holding on to a hot burning coal:

Imagine holding on to a hot burning coal. You would not fear letting go of it. In fact, once you noticed that you were holding on, you would probably drop it quickly. But we often do not recognise how we hold on to suffering. It seems to hold on to us. This is our practice: becoming aware of how suffering arises in our mind and of how we become identified with it, and learning to let it go.

Of course, there might be a very good reason for us to be angry. Being mindful of anger is not about resigning ourselves to situations where we are being exploited. Rather, it frees us from the added suffering we experience when we lack awareness of what is happening, and so let anger control our actions.

Strategies for managing aversion

- One way of working with the obstacle of aversion is to use the ABC of emotional first aid (page 157). This allows you to drop the story that is associated with the emotion, and simply be aware of the raw energy of aversion, becoming curious about it and allowing it to pass.
- Rather than unconsciously acting while in the heat of aversion, or trying to suppress it, you can allow it to be as it is, with the understanding that it will pass in its own time.
- Once the heat of the emotion has passed, you can deal with it in a constructive, more conscious way, using your calmer, more logical mind to find the best solution to the problem.

Another powerful way of managing aversion is to bring lovingkindness and compassion to the situation, which you will learn about in the final week (page 192).

Sleepiness

Many of us live in overdrive, so when we come to meditation we often discover the complete exhaustion that exists beneath our hyper-adrenalised state. Sometimes sleepiness is simply a sign that we're tired and need more rest, but it can be a disguised form of resistance, a tuning-out. Conversely, it can be the mind's response to the sudden lack of external stimulation that comes with meditation. Finally, sleepiness might be underpinned by boredom or a sense of futility, presenting as thoughts such as 'What's the point?' or 'I'll never be able to do this'.

Strategies for managing sleepiness

- Sit up.
- Open your eyes.
- Don't dress too warmly.
- Wash your face with cold water.
- Do a walking meditation until the sleepiness passes.
- Pay attention to one breath at a time to engage your attention.
- Bring curiosity to the experience of falling asleep. Try to notice the moment you shift from being awake to falling asleep.
- Have a nap. Sometimes sleepiness is just a sign we need more rest.

Restlessness

Restlessness can arise as physical or mental agitation. When physically restless we find it hard to get comfortable and we constantly fidget. A mental restlessness can manifest as worry or distraction, as a mind that has difficulty settling.

Restlessness of the mind can manifest in different ways. It can be experienced as many different thoughts grabbing at our attention, or it can be one particular thought that incessantly hijacks our attention. When you feel like you've been taken hostage by a single, constant thought, you can untangle yourself by quietly saying, 'I am having the thought that [insert thought here].' I've found that this technique helps me step back into being the observer of my thoughts. It also reminds me that thoughts are real, but not necessarily true, and through observing our thoughts we get less consumed by them. Labelling a thought reduces its impact.

Another helpful way to settle a distracted mind is to count the breaths up to ten at the beginning of each practice. It may also be helpful to pay attention to your restlessness and explore it outside of meditation. Spend a few moments writing about what you have observed and explore your feelings around the theme or issue. A valuable complement to meditation practice can be a mentor, therapist, or life coach to help you see beyond your blind spots and understand why the same theme keeps coming up in your practice.

Strategies for managing restlessness

- To address physical agitation, find out if there is an underlying physical pain that is causing the agitation, and if there is, find a more supportive posture to help alleviate the pain.
- Let the agitated energy flow by going for a walk or doing another form of exercise.
- Unfulfilled desires and cravings, along with dislikes or aversion that we are suppressing, can be underlying causes of restlessness, so turn to the emotional first-aid practice to uncover these.

Doubt

There are healthy forms of doubt, including **inquiring doubt**, which is the kind of questioning that helps us make sense of new information and challenge the truth of what we are taught. However, the type of doubt that is an obstacle to our progress is **reactive doubt**, a form of indecision that keeps us stuck, clouds our judgement and threatens to undermine our practice before we've even given it a chance.

Doubt can often arise in relation to your meditation practice, or even manifest as doubting your own capacity to meditate ('I'll never get this, it's too hard'). Maybe, after a few weeks of practice, you start wondering if it's just a waste of time.

As Yann Martel writes in his novel *Life of Pi*, 'To choose doubt as a philosophy of life is akin to choosing immobility as a means of transportation.'

Doubt is like a force that pulls the rug out from under you. It can paralyse you, and prevent you from progressing along the mindfulness path.

Strategies for managing doubt

- A powerful strategy to prevent doubt from derailing your practice is to create timelines and parameters to give yourself an opportunity to continue your learning and practice without being constantly undermined by your doubting mind
- Another strategy is to call upon faith, not in the religious sense, but in the form that Sharon Salzberg describes. 'Faith is a verb, an active willingness to suspend judgment and to see what is true for yourself.'

When doubt arises with its seductive force, direct your attention to the body and see what you notice. What emotions sit beneath doubt? Notice the tension associated with a need to 'work it all out', and use the outbreath to relax and bring some ease to your practice. When a cloud of doubt sets in, whether during meditation or simply in life, bring an active attitude of kindness and compassion to yourself. Remind yourself that wise decisions are not made under the spell of doubt. Wait until doubt has passed before making any final decisions.

There is a famous simile from the ancient Buddhist texts that Joseph Goldstein refers to in his book *Experience of Insight*. It describes all five of these mind states and how they obscure our clarity:

The mind that is unobscured by the hindrances can be likened to a pond of clear water. Desire is like the water becoming coloured with pretty dyes. We become entranced with the beauty and intricacy of the colour and so do not penetrate to the depths. Anger, ill will, aversion, are like boiling water. Water that is boiling is very turbulent. You can't see through to the bottom. This kind of turbulence in the mind, the violent reaction of hatred and aversion, is a great obstacle to understanding. Sloth and torpor is like the pond of water covered with algae, very dense. One cannot possibly penetrate to the bottom because you can't see through the algae. It is a very heavy mind. Restlessness and worry are like a pond when wind-swept. The surface of the water is agitated by strong winds. When influenced by restlessness and worry, insight becomes impossible because the mind is not centred or calm. Doubt is like the water when muddied; wisdom is obscured by murkiness and cloudiness.

These five mind states initially seem like they will prevent us from achieving the clarity and peace promised by meditation, yet they are actually the doorway to our freedom. They offer us grist for the mill in our mindfulness practice. These obstacles become opportunities to practise pausing and observing with wisdom, rather than getting lost in reactivity and confusion. Gil Fronsdal, an American meditation teacher, compares being lost in one of the obstacles to wandering through a maze with your eyes on the ground: 'Being mindful is like standing above the maze to get an overview. Mindfulness gives us better perspective of what is happening.'

Through shining the light of awareness on the challenges in our practice (and life), we discover that what may seem like an obstacle is actually a signpost along the path towards self-understanding, wisdom and happiness.

As Rainer Maria Rilke wrote:

How should we be able to forget those ancient myths that are at the beginning of all peoples, the myths about dragons that at the last moment turn into princesses; perhaps all the dragons of our lives are princesses who are only waiting to see us once beautiful and brave. Perhaps everything terrible is in its deepest being something helpless that wants help from us.

Whatever our choices in life, one thing we can be sure of is that along with the joys, we'll also face challenges. We can either meet these challenges with resistance and a sense that they are in the way of our happiness, or choose to live by the wisdom of stoic philosopher Marcus Aurelius and recognise that 'what's in the way, is the way'.

Congratulations on completing

WEEK THREE

What was the most common obstacle that came up in your meditation practice this week?

As you continue with your daily meditation practice, remember to apply the antidotes to each obstacle as they arise, and continue practising the mindful ABC of emotional first aid.

During one of the silent meditation retreats I attended, boredom was my regular 'visitor'. My teacher suggested that in the next meditation sitting, instead of trying to get away from the boredom, I could try to welcome it with curiosity.

'Next time you feel bored,' she advised, 'see if you can imagine you are a scientist and put your magnifying glass on the feeling of boredom in your body. How do you know you are bored? Are there particular feelings in your body that signal boredom? Where in your body do you feel boredom? In your head? Your chest? Your belly? Bring some curiosity to this experience of boredom and see what happens.'

Despite feeling sceptical, I decided to try it. Surprisingly, I noticed all kinds of sensations that I'd never noticed before. Ironically, the process of purposefully engaging with boredom actually transformed it into quite an interesting experience.

Jon Kabat-Zinn captured this instruction to move towards difficult emotions through his teaching of 'putting out the welcome mat' to everything that comes up in our meditation practice. This means that when difficult thoughts, emotions or body sensations arrive, rather than trying to push these experiences away, we allow things to be as they are, staying with what is happening with a kind, compassionate and open presence. Paradoxically, when we try to get rid of difficult thoughts or feelings, we actually end up keeping our attention focused on them, which keeps them alive longer. As we make space for difficult thoughts or feelings, they tend to come and go more easily.

On my encounter with boredom, rather than battling against a reality I didn't want to experience, I welcomed it and returned to paying careful attention to the present moment. Over time, I explored this practice with other difficult emotions such as tiredness, anger, fear, and sadness. I was fascinated to discover that simply paying mindful attention to my emotional states could profoundly transform them.

The way we pay attention changes our reality.

We can't control the feelings we have, just like we can't control the thoughts that happen to come into our mind, but we can control the relationship we have with our experience and our emotions. In mindfulness, we are asked to turn towards experience, and to be open to everything that arises, with curiosity, compassion and acceptance.

In this context, acceptance is not resignation. It is not about giving up or staying in a deeply problematic situation that you can't change. Rather, acceptance simply means not struggling with reality. Accepting whatever is happening is the first step to responding to it with wisdom and effectiveness.

The 13th-century Persian poet Rumi depicts this idea of 'putting out the welcome mat' and accepting all of our experience in his poem 'The Guest House':

This being human is a guest house.
Every morning a new arrival.
A joy, a depression, a meanness,
some momentary awareness comes
as an unexpected visitor.
Welcome and entertain them all!
Even if they are a crowd of sorrows,
who violently sweep your house
empty of its furniture,
still, treat each guest honourably.
He may be clearing you out
for some new delight.
The dark thought, the shame, the malice.
meet them at the door laughing and invite them in.
Be grateful for whatever comes.
because each has been sent
as a guide from beyond.

As we move into the final week of meditation, remember to put out the 'welcome mat' to all of the unexpected visitors that arrive at the doorstep of your daily practice.

HEART FOOD

Feed the source of your vital energy
with these healthy creations

We've long associated the heart with emotion. In fact, in ancient Egypt it was the heart, not the brain that was thought to be the source of wisdom, emotions, memory and the soul. Science may have since turned its attention to the brain and gut as our sources of intelligence, but the heart can still be a genuine signal of our emotional state – it beats faster when we're excited and aches when we feel sorrow. It's also functionally essential for our survival, and for the optimum functioning of our entire bodies, including our brains. So look after your heart with this week's recipes.

Spinach, basil & almond pesto

By Sun Hyland

www.neweartheating.com

Packed full of mono-unsaturated fats and antioxidants,
almonds serve to lower your risk of heart disease.
Research has also shown that almonds keep your cholesterol
levels in check.

½ bunch basil

100g baby spinach

4 cloves garlic, peeled and roughly chopped

1¼ cup olive oil

1 cup raw almonds

½ cup sunflower seeds

1½ tsp sea salt

½ tsp freshly cracked pepper

1 cup water

Soak the sunflower seeds in 1 cup of water for 1 hour, then
drain.

Lightly dry-toast the almonds in a heavy-based pan. Place them
in a food processor and pulse in several bursts until they have
broken up into nice little chunks. Don't overdo it – you don't
want the almonds to turn to powder. Remove from the food
processor and put aside.

Pick the leaves off the basil. Wash and spin dry. Also wash and
spin the spinach.

Place the garlic, cracked pepper, sunflower seeds and greens in the food processor. Add the salt and olive oil. Blend in bursts at first, then continuously for a minute or two until you achieve your desired consistency. Stir in the toasted almonds using a spatula.

Serve with salads, burgers, or pasta.

Raw vegan maqui berry cheesecake

By Amy Crawford
www.theholisticingredient.com

Blueberries are known to be antioxidant powerhouses. The key may be their large numbers of 'anthocyanins', the plant compound that gives them that rich, deep blue colour. Animal and cell studies have found that these anthocyanins cause blood vessels to relax and increase production of nitric oxide, which helps in maintaining normal blood pressure.

Crust

1 cup of almonds (or half almonds, half pistachios)

¾ cup fresh dates, pitted and chopped

¾ cup shredded coconut

1 heaped tbsp coconut oil, softened

½ cup cacao nibs

Filling

3 cups chopped cashews, soaked in filtered water for at least 3 hours

1 cup of blueberries (if using frozen, defrost them first)

1 cup strawberries (fresh is best)

½ cup coconut nectar (or maple syrup or rice malt syrup)

¾ cup coconut oil, melted

Juice of 1 lemon

2 tbsp maqui berry powder

1 tsp vanilla

Lightly grease a 20cm (8-inch) spring-form cake tin using coconut oil and line the bottom of the tin with baking paper.

To make the crust, add almonds, dates, shredded coconut, coconut oil and cacao nibs into a food processor and blend until well combined. Press the mixture evenly into the bottom of the cake tin and place in the fridge.

To make the filling, drain the cashews of excess water and rinse. Place into the food processor with coconut oil, coconut nectar, lemon juice and vanilla. Blend until silky smooth.

Remove half of the mixture from the food processor and set aside in a bowl.

Add the strawberries to the mixture in the food processor and combine. Pour the strawberry layer onto the crust. Lightly tap the tin on a firm surface to remove any small air bubbles. Place in the freezer for an hour until firm. The firmer the layer, the more defined the layering, so be patient.

Place the other half of the mixture with the blueberries and maqui berry powder into the food processor and combine until smooth. Pour on top of the strawberry layer. Lightly tap to remove any bubbles as above.

Place in the freezer until firm. Remove the whole cake from the pan while frozen and place on a serving platter. Defrost in the refrigerator or for an hour on the bench prior to serving.

Roast beetroot & blue cheese salad

Sun Hyland

www.neweartheating.com

Serves 4

Beets promote blood flow to your brain! They contain high concentrations of nitrates, which are converted into nitrites by bacteria in your mouth. Nitrites help open blood vessels in the body, increasing blood-flow to the brain and oxygenating the body. Sharpen your mind and your memory with a beetroot boost today.

500g beetroot

100g rocket

200g snow peas

150g blue cheese

30ml balsamic vinegar

60ml extra virgin olive oil

1 tsp salt

1 tsp freshly cracked pepper

Heat your oven to 200°C.

Slice the beetroot in half and then into wedges up to 1cm thick. Place on a baking tray with half the olive oil and half the salt; then rub the oil onto the beetroot with your hands. Pop into the oven for about an hour. Every 20 minutes or so, take the tray out and move the beetroot around a little so that it cooks evenly. Cook until a knife easily cuts through or, if you like, for a while longer, so it starts to get crispy.

While the beetroot is cooking, wash the snow peas and remove the tops and strings. Slice in half on an angle. If they're a little bit on the floppy side, leave them immersed in cold fresh water to bring some of their crunch back.

Wash and spin the rocket. Place in a salad bowl with the snow peas, vinegar, and remaining olive oil and salt. Mix gently.

When the beetroot is ready, allow it to cool slightly and then mix through the salad. Crumble half of the blue cheese through as well. The still-warm beetroot will melt the cheese a little, bringing out the flavour.

Serve onto plates and then crumble the remaining cheese on top.

Minty lemon & banana hotcakes

By Amy Crawford
www.theholisticingredient.com
Makes 2-3 small hotcakes

Mint has been used in holistic medicine for centuries to aid digestion and to alleviate stomach pains. It contains menthol, an organic compound that acts as a mild anaesthetic.

1 egg
A handful of fresh mint leaves
3 dessert spoons almond meal
1 dessert spoon coconut, flaked or desiccated
1 tsp grated lemon rind
½ a banana (whole if small)
1 heaped tsp coconut oil, for pan
Pinch of salt
Yoghurt of choice, to top

Place a small pan on the stove on medium heat. Throw all of the above ingredients (bar yoghurt and coconut oil) in a blender (stick will do) and blend until well-combined and smooth. Add the coconut oil to the pan when hot. Once melted, plop 2 pikelet-sized spoonfuls of the mixture into your pan and let them sit for about 2 minutes. Using a spatula gently check the underside – you want them to be golden before you turn them. When ready, flick them over and leave for a further 2 or so minutes. Pop them on a plate and top with a dollop of yoghurt

WEEK FOUR

Deepen foundations

of happiness

Grow positivity

'We try to fix the outside so much, but our control of the outer world is limited,
temporary, and often, illusory. Happiness is a state of inner fulfilment, not the
gratification of inexhaustible desires for outward things.'
Matthieu Ricard

We know that a large part of our potential happiness is determined by the state of our minds – what we think and where we focus our attention. A widely experienced obstacle to our happiness is the process of '**hedonic adaptation**'. This is the normal human tendency that allows us to 'get used to' both positive and negative events in our life. In the context of a negative event, it can be the basis of resilience, as we adapt to difficulties and regain our baseline happiness after the difficulty has passed.

However, hedonic adaptation also gets us used to positive and pleasant experiences, so much so that our enjoyment in or happiness from them lessens. Whether it's being in a long-term relationship, getting a promotion, winning the lottery or losing weight, over time we adapt to the positives in our lives and return to our baseline levels of happiness. To combat this, we need to actively cultivate practices that can maintain our appreciation and help us stay grateful for the things we so easily take for granted.

In this final week of *The Happiness Plan*, you'll be exploring two guided meditations. The first practice, the lovingkindness meditation, trains the mind and heart towards generosity, compassion and a sense of connection to those around you. The second meditation, the happiness meditation, is a powerful practice that helps you develop a clear vision for your own happiness. Along with the guided meditations, you'll find daily mindful practices that will deepen the foundations of your happiness, amplifying your gratitude and connection to those around you.

The lovingkindness meditation, traditionally called the *Metta* practice, is a simple but profoundly powerful one. It not only helps us develop compassion in our lives, but also acts as an antidote to the negative feelings we can experience towards ourselves or others.

In an interview with Sharon Salzberg, one of the world's leading insight meditation teachers, she explains:

> Sometimes lovingkindness is described as extending friendship to ourselves and others. I think of it as a type of self therapy, where we don't just develop self acceptance, but we also develop the skills to alchemise negative feelings towards others into compassion.

Lovingkindness is a form of love that is an ability, and, as research scientists have shown, it can be learned. It is the ability to look at ourselves and others with kindness instead of reflexive criticism; to include in our concern those to whom we normally pay no attention; to care for ourselves unconditionally instead of thinking, 'I will love myself as long as I never make a mistake.' It is the ability to gather our attention and really listen to others, even those we've written off as not worth our time. It is the ability to see the humanity in people we don't know and the pain in people we find difficult.

Although it felt awkward and forced for me initially, it has become a practice that nourishes me especially when I'm feeling depleted or despairing about the state of the world and the immense suffering that exists within it. As you progress with your mindfulness meditation practice, the lovingkindness practice becomes an essential ingredient to help you bring compassion to yourself when meeting the undesirable parts of yourself and maintain compassion for others when you experience their undesirable parts that can cause friction and tension within relationships. The practice asks us to expand beyond our own personal concerns and open to a larger perspective, which ultimately supports our happiness.

During the first year of my daughter's life, when multiple night wake-ups were the norm, and exhaustion was a permanent companion, I would turn to lovingkindness both for myself, my daughter and my partner at times when I felt overwhelmed by the demands. In the early morning hours, when my daughter cried, lovingkindness was an anchor and inner resource which filled me with strength, patience, energy and compassion.

In the lovingkindness meditation you are invited to connect with your own desire for happiness and activate this aspiration for yourself. Then as you move through the practice, you bring various people to mind and connect with their desire for happiness, sending them a wish that they, too, will experience a life of genuine happiness. The practice is an opportunity to pause and consciously bring kindness and compassion to ourselves and others. It's a beautiful way of reminding ourselves of the truth of our interdependence and interconnectedness. Through the practice, we connect with the universal desire for happiness and our shared vulnerability in the face of constant change.

The practice is another way of calming the mind. However, rather than anchoring our attention to our breath or thoughts, we anchor our attention to the phrases that we silently repeat to ourselves.

WEEK FOUR

Day One

THE LOVINGKINDNESS MEDITATION

'Talk to yourself like you would to someone you love.'
Brené Brown

When I was first introduced to the lovingkindness practice, I found it awkward and a bit forced. I didn't really understand the purpose of it and it never seemed to inspire any noticeably positive feelings. For a while I wondered if I was doing it correctly, or whether it was simply too airy-fairy for me. However, I decided to persist, following my teacher's advice to be patient. Over time, I discovered that the benefits of the practice were not only experienced *in the practice itself*, but also in my broader life, especially in the domain of relationships.

After a month I noticed that I'd developed a stronger sense of connection to everyone around me, and to strangers. I noticed I was less emotionally triggered by the challenging people in my life, whether at home or at work. I was able to access deeper compassion in the face

213

of conflict or tension with others, recognising that people's difficult behaviours were often an expression of their own inner wounds, rather than intentional personal attacks. My practice allowed me to recognise that, as Mother Teresa famously said, 'Some people come into our life as blessings and some as lessons.' Practising lovingkindness on a regular basis primes us to turn these interpersonal challenges into opportunities for growth.

In ancient Buddhist tradition, the lovingkindness meditation was practiced as an antidote to fear. It's definitely helped me become more courageous, particularly in situations involving other people. One example of this is public speaking. Just before big presentations, when I'm about to get on the stage and feel my nervousness peak, I send the audience lovingkindness. This always reminds me that the audience is a group of vulnerable human beings who, just like me, face challenges, fears and disappointments, and who just want to be happy. I feel more connected through our shared vulnerability, and it makes the experience far less threatening. Try out the guided lovingkindness meditation today and continue working with it for the next four days. Remember that you don't need to feel anything in particular: just follow the instructions and focus on the intention of wishing yourself and others happiness and wellbeing.

LOVINGKINDNESS MEDITATION GUIDANCE

Purpose

- To build our capacity for compassion and increase our sense of connection to others.
- To train the mind towards openness and kindness.
- To provide a circuit breaker for habitual modes of negative thinking.

The practice

- This meditation is best done in a comfortable and quiet place, where you can lie or sit comfortably.
- It involves silently repeating phrases of goodwill to yourself, to someone who has helped you, to someone who you know is suffering, to someone you don't know very well, and to a distant group of people.
- The guidance for this meditation stays close to the traditional wording. However, the idea of the lovingkindness meditation is to find words and phrases that feel comfortable and resonant for you. Feel free to change the words of this guided meditation to suit your own style.

Tips

- It's not so much about creating a particular feeling of love or kindness in yourself, but rather bringing an *intention* to creating more self-compassion and kindness.
- If you find your attention wandering, don't worry – that's what the mind will do. Once you recognise that it has wandered off, gently let go of the distractions and bring your focus back to the phrases.

You can listen to the lovingkindness meditation by visiting www.mindlifeproject.com/book

A condensed transcript of the practice is included below in case you'd prefer to read it and guide yourself through.

Lovingkindness meditation guidance

1. Bring awareness to the body, becoming aware of the sensations of the body sitting. Notice any areas of tension, and with each outbreath release the tension and allow the body to soften.

2. Become aware of the feeling of the breath.

3. Move your attention to the area of the heart, bringing awareness to this area and noticing any sensations.

4. We begin the lovingkindness practice by bringing a sense of kindness and compassion to ourselves, acknowledging our desire to live this one precious life with deep happiness, health and fulfilment.

5. Repeat the following phrases to yourself silently, or adjust them to be more meaningful to you:

   May I be happy.
   May I be healthy.
   May I be safe.
   May I live with ease.

6. Some people find it helpful to link the words to the breath. While breathing in, silently say to yourself, 'May I be ...' Then breathing out, '... happy'.

7. Now, bring to mind someone who has supported you. It could be a family member, a friend or a mentor. Allow an image of this person to come to mind. If visualising is difficult, you can silently think of their name.

8. Bring an intention of kindness and well wishes to them through repeating the below phrases, using the breath as an anchor to the words if it is helpful:

   May you be happy.
   May you be healthy.
   May you be safe.
   May you live with ease.

9. With the next outbreath, allow the image or thoughts of this person to dissolve. Bring to mind someone who is suffering. Offer the phrases of kindness and compassion to them:

   May you be happy.
   May you be healthy.

May you be safe.

May you live with ease.

10. Allow the image of this person to dissolve and bring to mind someone who you see now and then, but who is more distant – a shop owner, or an acquaintance. Acknowledge that though you don't know their particular story, just like you, they desire happiness and are vulnerable to the constant change that comes with being human. Use the breath to support the phrases:

May you be happy.

May you be healthy.

May you be safe.

May you live with ease.

11. Extend the field of this lovingkindness to include people or groups of people in the world who are suffering in this moment, whether through natural disaster, war, or poverty, knowing that just like you these people wish to be free from suffering and live in safety. With each breath, send the intention of kindness and compassion beyond the boundaries of space and time, to include all people, known and unknown, close and far:

May all beings be happy.

May all beings be healthy.

May all beings be safe.

May all beings live with ease.

TODAY'S PRACTICE
Use lovingkindness throughout your day

This week, alongside the guided meditation, you can weave this practice into the ordinary experiences in your day. You don't have to include the whole script when you do the practice. Instead you can apply the phrases in a shorter version to specific people of your choice. Simply tune in to your breath for a few moments and then bring these phrases to mind in relation to challenging situations or feelings.

Below are nine situations where you could experiment with shorter, self-guided lovingkindness meditations. Try a few of them out as you move through your day.

Some opportunities to practice lovingkindness

1. After having an emotionally charged conversation with a friend or family member.
2. While waiting for a medical test to come back.
3. When feeling angry.
4. When waiting in a queue (supermarkets, airports, traffic lights) and feeling frustration.
5. When walking down the street (silently send an intention of lovingkindness to a stranger who passes you by).
6. On public transport at peak hour (find the most stressed-looking person and send it to them).
7. Before a difficult conversation with your boss or an employee.
8. When your child is testing your patience and pressing your emotional buttons.
9. When you encounter someone struggling with homelessness.

WHAT THE RESEARCH TELLS US
ABOUT LOVINGKINDNESS

One study demonstrated that just seven minutes of lovingkindness meditation was enough to improve meditators' good feelings, including a greater sense of calm, connection and happiness in life. Two-and-a-half hours of lovingkindness made people feel more relaxed and more likely to donate to charity.

Day Two

SOAK UP PLEASANT MOMENTS

'Drop by drop is the water pot filled. Likewise, the wise man,
gathering it little by little, fills himself with good.'
The Buddha

How was your first lovingkindness meditation yesterday?

As we've been exploring throughout this book, the way we pay attention in our lives profoundly affects what we notice and how we feel. Bringing more conscious attention to the positive moments in our life is one way to enhance our happiness. At our most basic, biological level, we're much more sensitive to the things that pose a potential danger or threat to us than to pleasant things. Our brain is constantly scanning the environment, determining what is safe and what is harmful, and we are wired to notice and remember negative experiences more than positive ones. This design feature of the brain is called the 'negativity bias', a helpful concept that explains why we're so much more affected by small, negative events than by positive ones.

Our brain's negativity bias robs us of moments that could be used to build happiness and positivity.

Psychologist and *New York Times* bestselling author Rick Hanson summed up the negativity bias with a simple metaphor:

> *'The brain is like Velcro for bad experiences and*
> *Teflon for positive ones.'*

The good news is that we can update the inner software of the brain to help support greater happiness in life and overcome the effect of this negativity bias. During a conversation I had with Rick, he explained:

Changing the brain for the better is a two-stage process in which activated mental 'states' must get installed as lasting 'traits'. Almost all positive traits – like happiness, or gratitude, or feeling loved, or having compassion, or being determined to succeed at work, or being more skilful with other people – start with a positive state. That's been under our nose all along, but it has radical implications.

But, if we're in a positive state and we don't install it in the brain, it's wasted. It's a momentarily pleasant feeling, but has no lasting value. That's why taking the extra ten to twenty seconds to stay with the experience, to try to feel it in the body and have it be as rich as possible, is key to turning positive mental states into lasting positive mental traits. The accumulation of these little moments will gradually change your brain for the better.

A powerful mindfulness technique described in Rick's book *Hardwiring Happiness* is called '**taking in the good**', which helps us balance out the brain's negativity bias. See if you can incorporate this practice into your day today, and notice how it affects your mood. I've found it to be genuinely transformative.

TODAY'S PRACTICE
Taking in the good

Commit to noticing the pleasant passing moments in your day by being mindful of pleasant experiences.

1. When you're having a pleasant moment (it can be something really small, like the feeling of warm water in the shower, or the taste of a chocolate, or the smile of your child, or the feeling of sun on your body), consciously recognise it as a pleasant moment and soak it up through your senses.
2. Notice that you're experiencing pleasure and stay with that feeling for ten to twenty seconds.
3. Explore what it feels like physically. Does your body feel relaxed or tense?
4. Continue on with your day.

By doing this you are transforming those momentary emotional states into longer-lasting 'traits' that will support wellbeing and happiness.

As a mother with a small child and a business, my life can be busy, and I've found that it's easy for pleasant moments to pass by unnoticed in the chaos of it all. By 'taking in the good' I am able to savour those moments more often. On a recent holiday, I watched my daughter delight in splashing water in a bucket and collecting stones on the beach. The sun warmed my back, the colours were vibrant and the sound of waves crashed in the background. I consciously paused to take this moment in, to capture and absorb it fully in my body and mind, relishing it and soaking it up into every cell. Taking time to soak up pleasant experiences using our senses makes life so much richer. It also helps us appreciate what we have, which is the foundation for gratitude and deep happiness.

Day Three

INCREASE YOUR DAILY DIET
OF POSITIVE EMOTIONS

'Your mind will take the shape of what you frequently hold in thought.'
Marcus Aurelius

For the past few days we've looked at how we can use mindfulness to shift our perspective and increase our overall happiness. It might seem obvious that having more positive feelings will make you feel happier, but what's interesting is how these feelings can actually affect our physical health. In her groundbreaking work, world-leading positive psychology researcher Barbara Fredrickson discovered that positive emotions can actually improve our cardiovascular health.

In Week Two you were introduced to the vagus nerve (page 93), the main nerve that is part of your parasympathetic (or 'rest and digest') nervous system. The vagus nerve, which in Latin means '*wandering*', runs through the entire body, starting at the brain stem just behind the ears and travelling down both sides of the neck through the chest and abdomen. Its role is to integrate information from the internal organs and the brain. So the stronger the activity of this vagus nerve, the better our bodies are at calming down after stress.

The strength of your vagus nerve activity is called your 'vagal tone', and this can be measured by an electrocardiogram (ECG) machine, which records the rhythms of your heart. It is a sign of your overall health and is linked to better cardiovascular health, glucose regulation and immune functioning. Barbara Fredrickson and her team have discovered that people who experience more frequent positive emotions not only feel happier and more connected to others, but, as she explains, 'The rhythms of their hearts become more efficient and healthy, with an increase in vagal tone.'

Frederickson has also found that increasing your positive emotions helps to increase creativity and allows for better brain function:

One of the things we've learnt through laboratory experiments is that if you inject a mild positive emotion into somebody's experience, maybe even just have them socialise with somebody for a short stretch or show a fun movie or something, that fundamentally changes the way the mind works – the way the brain works. People are able to take in more information. It broadens people's awareness. Our peripheral vision literally expands when we are experiencing a mild positive state, and that enables people to see the bigger picture, step back and connect the dots between diverse ideas. That's one of the in-the-moment benefits of positive emotions, that they help us break with typical thinking and come up with creative solutions.

Living such fast-paced lives, we tend to forget to do things that are purely about bringing us joy and pleasure. With increasing societal pressure to work hard, many of us feel we don't have the time for it, or we feel guilty carving out space for pleasure when there is an endless list of tasks to complete. However, Fredrickson's research makes it clear that doing things for pure joy and pleasure should not be seen as a luxury, but as a prescription for our mental and physical wellbeing. Just as we need to eat a balanced diet, ensuring we regularly receive nutrients that nourish us, we have to regularly prioritise activities that bring us the joy and connection that nourish us on a deeper level. As Fredrickson explained in a conversation for Mindful in May:

> Just like eating one stem of broccoli in a year isn't going to make you healthy, we need to have quite a few positive emotions in our daily experiences to feel the effects. They shouldn't be rare. They shouldn't be something that we save for a vacation. They need to be part of what we ingest every day.

TODAY'S PRACTICE
Schedule a boost in positive emotions

Today take some time to brainstorm a list of ten ideas that you could schedule into your week to boost your daily diet of positive emotions. Print this list out and stick it on your fridge to remind you of the importance of finding time to do things that make you feel happy.

As well as scheduling in time to do things that will bring you happiness, try out this letter-writing exercise as a way of generating positive emotions.

It can be easy to acknowledge the good in others, but today take some time to think about the good within yourself. Try this practice with a playful, light-hearted attitude. Write a letter to yourself as if you were writing to a friend to acknowledge what you most value and admire about them.

Write a letter to yourself

1. Start the letter with 'Dear [insert your own name]'.

2. Set a timer for five minutes and let your pen flow. Write about the strengths you most value about yourself – moments of generosity, courage, forgiveness, or times you moved out of your comfort zone in order to expand and grow. As you write, be mindful of any thoughts, feelings or bodily sensations that come up from moment to moment.

3. Notice any resistance to doing this practice, or any scepticism you feel. Remember that it's just an experiment – and an opportunity to explore what it's like to bring kindness to yourself – so try it out with an open mind and playful heart.

4. Keep this letter and refer back to it from time to time, to support your daily diet of positive emotions and wellbeing.

WEEK FOUR

Day Four

CONNECT WITH NATURE

'Nature's peace will flow into you as sunshine flows into trees.
The winds will blow their own freshness into you, and the storms
their energy, while cares will drop off like autumn leaves.'
John Muir

How did your practice go yesterday?

Did you manage to try the letter-writing exercise?

If you're feeling that you'd like to practise for longer periods of time, you could do two meditations back-to-back today, or set a timer and just sit without guidance.

If you live in the city, as I do, it can be easy to forget about the power of nature to generate positive emotions. Today, take some time to reflect on your calendar and commit to scheduling some time in nature. Although intuitively we know nature is good for us, there is a large body of scientific evidence to support the saying that 'green is good'.

- A study by Rachel and Stephen Kaplan revealed that 'office workers with a view of nature liked their jobs more, enjoyed better health and reported greater life satisfaction'.

- Roger S Ulrich, director of the Center for Health Systems and Design at Texas A&M University, conducted a famous study which found that nature can help the body heal. He discovered that patients who were recovering from abdominal surgery that had views of trees had easier recoveries, needed less pain medication and had fewer complications than those whose rooms faced brick walls.

- David Strayer, cognitive psychologist at the University of Utah, demonstrated that after three days of wilderness backpacking a group of participants performed fifty per cent better on creative problem-solving tasks. He called this the 'three-day effect' and described it as a kind of cleaning of the mental windshield that occurs when we've been immersed in nature long enough.

- Finally, a Stanford-led study has found that walking in nature could lower the risk of depression. The study, published in *Proceedings of the National Academy of Science*, found that people who walked for ninety minutes in a natural area, as opposed to participants who walked in a high-traffic urban setting, showed decreased activity in a region of the brain associated with depression.

For millennia, Indigenous Australians have recognised the power of nature to help anchor us in the present, supporting our wellbeing and wisdom. The traditional practice of '*dadirri*' is a way to incorporate mindfulness into our experience of nature, and gives us a sense of our interconnectedness with all things. Aboriginal writer Miriam Rose Ungunmerr-Baumann describes the practice:

Dadirri is inner, deep listening and quiet, a still awareness. *Dadirri* recognises the deep spring that is inside us. We call on it and it calls to us. It is something like what you call 'contemplation'. When I experience *dadirri*, I am made whole again. I can sit on the riverbank or walk through the trees; even if someone close to me has passed away, I can find my peace in this silent awareness. There is no need for words. A big part of *dadirri* is listening. In our Aboriginal way, we learned to listen from our earliest days. This was the normal way for us to learn. We learned by watching and listening, waiting and then acting. Our people have passed on this way of listening for over 40,000 years… There is no need to reflect too much and to do a lot of thinking. It is just being aware.

TODAY'S PRACTICE
Connect with nature

Today set aside five or ten minutes to connect deeply with nature, inspired by the practice of *dadirri*.

1. Choose something specific in nature to focus on. It could be a bird, a flower, a blade of grass, the ocean, a cloud, or you could go on a nature walk and let something capture your attention.
2. Spend some time being with this natural object. Connect initially with your own breath and body, and then bring your attention to the object of your choice. Just relax and allow yourself to be still and silent in the presence of this natural object.
3. Following this quiet mindful practice, you may feel moved to express the experience in some way. Journal about what it felt like,

write a poem to nature, or imagine you are the object you were focusing on. Perhaps draw something, or paint.

4. Remember to arrive at the process with no pressure to do or create, but rather to allow yourself time to simply be with nature. If something creative comes, see it as a bonus.

A TIP FOR CONNECTING WITH NATURE

In this modern world it can be so easy to forget our connection to nature. Just like the cycles of nature that constantly change, the rhythm of the breath is always changing. During your meditation this week, remember that you breathe in oxygen received from the trees around you, and you breathe out carbon dioxide, sustaining nature with your breath. In this way you can sense the very direct connection you have with nature.

Day Five

HAPPINESS MEDITATION

'Action without vision is only passing time, vision without action is merely day dreaming, but vision with action can change the world.'
Nelson Mandela

Today we move to our final meditation: the happiness meditation. This guided practice gives you an opportunity to reflect on your life and create a vision for your deepest happiness. I like to do this meditation regularly throughout the year, as a way of staying anchored to the things that are most important to me.

Even if you already have a vision for your own flourishing, this practice offers you a way of reflecting on and reimagining what will truly make you happy. If, while practising this meditation, your vision seems unclear or nothing comes to mind, just allow that to be as it is. Sometimes the mind needs more time and space to ponder these important questions. Be patient and try the practice for a few days in a row.

As someone who has always been sensitive to the reality of impermanence and the fact of our mortality, I've been obsessively driven to make my life as meaningful as possible. My vision of a happy life has always been inextricably linked to making a positive difference in the world. I want to help alleviate the suffering of those who are living with external hardships, including the consequences of poverty, or those who are suffering from inner hardships.

One aspect of our happiness is a sense that we are living a life of purpose. However, many of us struggle to work out what that purpose might be. A question that can often illuminate our direction in life is 'What issue in the world makes you angry?' The purpose of your life's work can then be to develop solutions to this issue.

For me, that issue is global poverty and the suffering of human beings who are living without their most basic needs: water, food, health care.

As Nelson Mandela wisely wrote, 'Poverty is not an accident. Like slavery and apartheid, it is man-made and can be removed by the actions of human beings.'

While travelling through the developing world and witnessing the most profound levels of poverty first-hand, I was filled with despair and an inner sense of responsibility. I was unwilling to be a bystander.

My own family story perhaps explains this drive and refusal to be passive in a world where millions suffer on a daily basis from a myriad of injustices. I remember, at about the age of ten, hearing the tragic stories of my grandparents who went through the Holocaust. In a family of nine siblings, my grandmother was the only survivor, and my grandfather lost his parents, wife, four-year-old child and siblings in the Holocaust. In my ten-year-old innocence, I asked my grandmother if people in the world knew what was happening at that time. She explained that they did and this confused me. How was it possible that people were aware of these unimaginable atrocities of genocide, yet didn't act to stop it? As I grew up, I understood how commonly idealism shrinks and complacency grows as we are consumed by our own personal concerns and the daily demands of work or family.

Meditation helps dissolve the artificial boundaries between ourselves and others, enhancing our compassion and sense of being part of a larger whole. In a famous letter dated 1950, a decade after World War II, Albert Einstein wrote:

> A human being is part of the whole, called by us 'Universe', a part limited in time and space. He experiences himself, his thoughts and feelings, as something separated from the rest – a kind of optical delusion of his consciousness. This delusion is a kind of prison for us, restricting us to our personal desires and to affection for a few persons nearest us. Our task must be to free ourselves from this prison by widening our circles of compassion.

The lovingkindness meditation you've been practising this week helps expand our circle of compassion, and in doing so, it expands the vision we have for our own lives. Rather than limiting ourselves to a myopic aspiration to improve our own existence, we find we can simultaneously expand our happiness and explore how to be of service to others. Paradoxically, as we contribute to the happiness of others, we are nourished with deeper meaning and purpose in our own lives.

In today's happiness meditation, you are invited to use your imagination and paint a picture of your life as it would be if it were fulfilling the greatest vision of your happiness. You'll begin by imagining what you need in order to fulfil your own basic survival needs, and then explore how you could use your own unique gifts, passions and strengths to contribute to the world and nourish a sense of deep fulfilment.

Practise this guided happiness meditation for the remaining three days of this month, in addition to any of the meditations we have explored over the past few weeks.

HAPPINESS MEDITATION GUIDANCE

Purpose

- To bring greater presence and awareness into your life.
- To consciously connect with what matters most and use it to form a vision for your future.
- To cultivate the attitude and practices you need in order to fulfil your desires for happiness and to allow you to flourish.

The practice

- Find a comfortable position lying down, or sitting in a chair.
- This practice takes you on a vision quest, picturing your ideal future and connecting with a sense of deep purpose.
- You are encouraged to use your imagination and be playful as you explore the ingredients required for a flourishing life.

Tips

- Sometimes our rational, logical mind tries to limit our imagination and obstruct the vision by protesting and convincing us that 'that isn't possible'. See if during this meditation, you can really allow your imagination to be in charge and not limit your vision to what your logical mind thinks is possible.

**You can listen to the happiness meditation by visiting
www.mindlifeproject.com/book**

A condensed transcript of the practice is included
below in case you'd prefer to read it and guide yourself
through.

This meditation has been inspired by my retreats with
Alan B Wallace.

Happiness meditation guidance

1. Take a few moments to connect with the breath.

2. Scan through the body and let go of any tightness or
   tension with each outbreath.

3. It can be easy in the busyness of life to forget to connect
   with what matters most, so allow any concerns from the
   day to dissolve as you become present and still.

4. Bring particular attention to the face. Allow your eyes to
   be soft, let your jaw relax, and bring your attention to the
   heartspace. It's easy to get disconnected from this area of
   the body, as we spend so much of our day in our heads.
   Gently rest your hand on your heart to sense this area of the
   body for a few moments.

5. Having tuned in to the heart, allow yourself to
   contemplate these questions: What is your vision for
   your deepest happiness and flourishing? What would

bring you deep fulfilment, meaning and happiness, now and into the future?

6. As you breathe from moment to moment, notice what images, words or thoughts come to mind as you contemplate this question: What is your vision for your greatest happiness? In other words, once your material needs are met – of food, shelter and wellbeing – what is it that would make you genuinely happy?

7. Allow your imagination to flow, and if nothing comes to mind, just rest with the flow of the breath, resting your attention on the sensations in the area of the heart and listening deeply.

8. Ask again, what would bring you greatest happiness? Imagine into the future. What does it look like?

9. Allow each outbreath to fill this vision with life, imagining this vision as a reality, here and now. With each breath, bring a wish to yourself: May this vision come to life.

10. In order to fulfil this vision, you may need to receive things from those around you, or from the world. So contemplate the next question: What would you love to receive from the world, from people near or far, in order to fulfil your greatest vision of happiness?

11. Imagine, with each inbreath, everything that you need flowing towards you from all directions.

12. Now, reflect on the fact that fulfilling your deepest vision of happiness will likely require an inner

transformation. Take a few moments to contemplate what attitudes, behaviours or qualities would support you to flourish.

13. Now, consider what qualities or behaviours you would like to let go of that may be getting in the way of your happiness.

14. Take a moment to recognise that, just like you, all human beings want to be free from suffering and live a life of happiness. So in the spirit of connection to all fellow human beings and the world at large, reflect on this last question: What could you offer the world that would call upon your greatest gifts, strengths and passions to contribute to the happiness of others? With each outbreath, allow your imagination to explore what you could offer the world.

15. Now letting go of this vision, bring your attention back to the breath, to this life force that infuses you with energy and possibility.

16. And in closing this practice, bring to mind anything you feel grateful for, no matter how big or small: anything that brings you happiness and offers you a sense of gratitude.

17. As the practice comes to a close, remember that you can tap into this reservoir of gratitude to fill you up with positive emotions and support your happiness and flourishing.

Day Six

PRACTISING GRATITUDE

*'Acknowledging the good that you already have in your
life is the foundation for all abundance.'*
Eckhart Tolle

How was the guided happiness meditation?

While projecting into the future is a powerful way to consciously move our lives towards fulfilment, it's important to notice the things in our lives that already bring us joy.

Mindfulness helps us pay deeper attention to the ordinary 'miracles' in our lives that we so often take for granted. In Week One you learned about the incredible complexity that is required for us to simply see, hear, smell, taste and feel, and perhaps you found that your gratitude and appreciation were sparked in response.

As we recognise the goodness and beauty that already fill our lives, through regularly acknowledging the good, we build new neural pathways that incline the mind towards the positive aspects of our existence. A study by Dr Joshua Brown, professor of psychological brain sciences at Indiana University, looked at the benefits of gratitude for three hundred students who were receiving counselling for depression or anxiety. The students were divided into three groups, the first writing a weekly letter of gratitude to another person (most participants didn't actually send it); the second writing about their negative feelings and experiences; and the third serving as a control group who did no writing activity. Both one month and three months after the writing exercise ended, those who wrote gratitude letters reported significantly better mental health than either of the other groups.

Gratitude isn't about denying the challenges or suffering in life. It's about amplifying the goodness that is already there by simply noticing it more consciously.

There has been a huge amount of research around the benefits of gratitude. Sonja Lyubomirsky, one of the world's leading positive psychologists, discovered that people who noted down what they were grateful for on a regular basis experienced not only an increase in happiness, but also improved physical health. On top of that, she found evidence that writing a letter of gratitude to someone boosts your happiness levels even if you don't send it.

Gratitude is also a powerful antidote to toxic emotions. Robert Emmons, a gratitude researcher, demonstrated that regular gratitude reduced feelings of envy and resentment. Emmons also discovered that for people who were experiencing chronic illness and pain, regular gratitude practice provided more positive emotions, better sleep, more connection and a more optimistic outlook on life.

TODAY'S PRACTICE
Boost Your Gratitude

Practise the gratitude spiral

Start by bringing attention to yourself, noticing both your body and your mind. Take a moment to bring to mind all of the different organs and systems in your body, and show gratitude to each of them. Thank the lungs for breathing, the heart for beating, the liver for cleansing and detoxifying, the digestive tract, the brain, the kidneys, the spleen, the nervous system, the skin – so many systems working every minute of every day to keep us alive. Then expand your awareness and bring to mind other people in your life and take a moment to be grateful for those who care for and support you. Then expand your awareness and bring attention to the world at large, connecting with what makes you feel grateful in your environment. You can run through this gratitude spiral each night before you go to sleep, or when you wake up in the morning.

Create a gratitude group to stay connected to the practice

I have participated in a gratitude group for a few years now and it's been a powerful way to stay connected to the goodness in my life. Contact a few friends and hold one another accountable to check in regularly and share something you feel grateful for. You could create a Facebook group, or use WhatsApp or another messaging service.

Start a gratitude journal

Keep a weekly diary where you record things that you're grateful for. Reflect on three such things from your day so far and then three things you are looking forward to. (Interestingly, research by Sonja Lyubomirsky reveals that choosing a single day once a week to practice gratitude has a greater impact on happiness levels than writing something down every day. In other words, it's important to keep a gratitude practice fresh and novel to avoid it becoming a meaningless task that you tack onto your day.)

Start a gratitude jar

This exercise is particularly effective with children, as it's a visual representation of gratitude. Find a large jar and get some small coloured pieces of paper. Choose one dinner or evening a week – ideally at the end of the week – and ask everyone to add a note of gratitude to the jar reflecting on five things for which you are grateful. At the end of the year sit down as a family, empty the gratitude jar and read through your many moments of gratitude.

Write a letter of gratitude to someone who has been kind to you

Research by Martin Seligman, pioneer of the positive psychology movement, demonstrates that people who write a letter to someone they appreciate increase their own levels of happiness for a month after giving the letter to the person. Make a habit of writing one gratitude letter a month to someone who has supported you, and where possible, try to actually send it!

Day Seven

CREATE A VISION FOR YOUR HAPPINESS

'Half of the soul's work is to be. The other half is to be of use.
It's in our nature to try with all our heart, at everything and anything,
until we chance to inhabit grace and come alive. And being so alive,
we become a conduit for life and a resource for others.'
Mark Nepo

As a child, some of my favourite books were from the *Choose Your Own Adventure* series. In these books, you were able to make choices on behalf of the protagonist that changed the course of the story. There were multiple endings – some happy, some scary – and you never knew exactly where your decisions would take you. I remember the delight of seeing the direction of the story shift according to my decisions. It gave me a sense of empowerment and agency.

Feeling empowered is such a crucial ingredient of happiness. One of the most depleting feelings we can have is a sense that we are stuck and unable to direct our own story. Whether we're feeling unsatisfied in our relationships or our careers, if we want to change our future we first need to get clearer about what we want that future to look like.

Through actively taking time to tune in to what we want our lives to look like, we can make decisions that move us closer to that vision. Mindfulness meditation offers us the space to inquire into what we really want for ourselves, and it helps us tune in to our inner guide as we map out where we want our lives to go.

TODAY'S PRACTICE
Mindful Visioning

Alfred Nobel, the inventor of dynamite, had an unexpected wake-up call late in his life – one that profoundly changed his sense of purpose and contribution to the world. Nobel was for many years an unpopular public figure, shunned for an invention that led to the destruction and loss of so many lives. In 1888, his older brother Ludvig, a famous engineer and successful businessman, fell ill and died. As the news spread, journalists mistakenly believed it was Alfred who had died. The story goes that Alfred woke up one day to see his own obituary in the papers, and it was a damning account of his life. The journalists reflected on the destruction and death that resulted from his invention. Shocked, Alfred began to reflect on what kind of human being he wanted to be. He decided to set up the Nobel Peace Prize and donated most of his fortune to the award.

Today, as a way of reflecting on the vision you have for yourself, take time to imagine that you've reached the end of your life, and write your own obituary as you would like it to be. How do you want to be remembered? Although reflecting on our own mortality may seem morbid, taking a moment to consider our own death can wake us up to the preciousness of our life and to how we want to live it. As the poet Mary Oliver asked, 'Tell me, what is it you plan to do with your one wild and precious life?'

In this obituary, you can paint a picture of the life you have lived, reflecting upon all its different aspects:

- Family.
- Career.
- Your biggest accomplishments.
- Your greatest contributions.
- What you stood for as a person.
- What most mattered to you.

This retrospective reflection on your life may give you a clearer perspective on what really matters.

SOUL FOOD

Recipes handpicked to nourish your body
and nurture your soul

This week ends the month with simple recipes that are intended to help you increase your daily dose of positive emotions. They are special treats that you can enjoy as an occasional addition to your daily life. Can you tell I have a sweet tooth?

Honey tahini cashew cookies

Amy Crawford

www.theholisticingredient.com

Makes approximately 18

1½ cups cashew meal*

½ cup white sesame seeds

⅓ cup white tahini

¼ cup raw honey

1 tbsp coconut oil, melted

1 tsp vanilla extract or vanilla powder

½ tsp baking soda

½ tsp cinnamon, ground

¼ tsp sea salt

Preheat oven to 175°C. Line a baking tray with baking paper.

In a large mixing bowl place cashew meal, baking soda, cinnamon and salt. In a small mixing bowl, combine tahini, raw honey, vanilla extract and coconut oil. Add the wet ingredients to the dry mix and use your hands to combine the dough. It should be slightly tacky to touch. Roll into balls of 2cm diameter.

Place the sesame seeds into a shallow dish. Roll balls in sesame seeds, then place onto baking tray. Press down to ½ cm thickness.

Bake for 10 minutes. If you would like even crispier cookies, flip and bake for a further 5 minutes. Allow to cool and store in an airtight container.

* To make cashew meal, blend raw cashews until they resemble coarse flour. Do not over-process otherwise the biscuits will not hold their shape in the oven.

Paleo sticky date pudding

Merry Maker sisters

www.themerrymakersisters.com

Serves 12

Pudding

1½ cups almond meal

1 cup chopped pitted dates

1 cup boiling water

⅓ cup coconut sugar

2 eggs

2 tbsp butter

1 tsp 100 per cent vanilla extract

1 tsp baking powder (optional)

Caramel sauce

1 cup coconut cream

⅓ cup coconut sugar

2 tbsp butter

1 tsp 100% vanilla extract

Preheat oven to 180°C (350°C) and line a 20cm cake tin with baking paper. In a bowl, place the dates and boiling water. Leave these to soak until the dates become soft.

Meanwhile, cream the coconut sugar and butter in a mixmaster until a paste forms. Add the eggs and vanilla extract, mix until combined.

In a separate bowl, mix the almond meal, baking powder and date/water mixture together. Add the butter/sugar batter and mix until combined.

Transfer the batter to the prepared cake tin and place into the oven for 45 minutes until lightly golden.

Allow to cool for 10 minutes before turning out on to a wire rack.

For the caramel sauce

In a medium-heat saucepan melt the butter and sugar together. Add the coconut cream and vanilla and continue to stir for 5 minutes. Be careful to not let it boil! Stir until nice and smooth.

To serve

Cut a slice of sticky date and pour the caramel sauce over the top!

Salted crunchy peanut butter & banana popsicles

By Amy Crawford

www.theholisticingredient.com

Serves 4

1 large banana

¾ cup yoghurt (natural, Greek or coconut)

½ cup organic crunchy peanut butter*

½ tsp Celtic sea salt

Place the banana, yoghurt and salt into a high-powered blender and pulse until smooth. Now add ¼ cup peanut butter and pulse just enough to combine the 'ice-cream' so that you don't lose the peanut crunch. Using a knife, scrape the remaining peanut butter into the popsicle holders, against the sides (I scraped 4 to 5 teaspoons-full into each popsicle, if that helps). Pour in the yoghurt mix, add a popsicle stick, place in your freezer and leave overnight or several hours at least. To remove, simply run the popsicle holder under hot water so that you can dislodge the popsicles.

Optional: Dunk in chocolate!

* If you don't like crunchy peanut butter, smooth will work too.

Beetroot, quinoa & chocolate muffins

By Amy Crawford
www.theholisticingredient.com
Makes 10–12 muffins

1½ cups water

1 cup uncooked quinoa

1 cup coconut sugar (if you have a low-sugar diet, don't be afraid to reduce this to ½–¾ cup)

1 cup cacao powder

¾ cup raw beetroot, grated

¾ cup organic butter, melted (you could also use coconut oil, though do know it will a lot more dense and heavy)

⅓ cup coconut milk

4 eggs

1½ tsp baking powder

½ tsp baking soda

½ tsp Celtic or Himalayan salt

Seeds of one vanilla pod (or 1 tsp vanilla essence)

Preheat your oven to 180°C. Line a 12-hole muffin tin with baking paper.

Rinse your quinoa thoroughly. Bring the quinoa and water to the boil on your stove. Cover, reduce heat and let simmer for ten minutes. Turn off the heat and leave the covered saucepan on the stove, lid on, for a further 10 minutes. Fluff with a fork and let it sit to cool.

Combine the coconut milk, eggs and vanilla in a blender. Add 2⅓ cups of cooked quinoa, butter, grated beetroot, coconut sugar, salt, baking powder, baking soda and cacao powder. Blend again until combined.

Bake in the centre of the oven for 30 minutes or until a skewer comes out clean. I recommend checking them at 20 minutes to make sure the tops are not burning – if they are, place a piece of baking paper over the top of the tray. Remove from the oven and cool in the pan before turning out onto a wire rack.

Those I haven't eaten, I keep frozen for a rainy day. They are of course *amazing* fresh out of the oven, but I like to extend the pleasure of my creations.

CONCLUSION

'Joy is the happiness that doesn't depend on what happens.'
Brother David Steindl-Rast

A group of scientists were digging in the hot, remote town of Afar in Ethiopia. It was 1974 and The Beatles were playing on a cassette player as the scientists searched the earth for bones that might expand our collective understanding of human evolution. Suddenly, the lead paleoanthropologist, Donald Johanson, hit on what he thought was an elbow bone. Johanson kept digging and found half of a skeleton. He had discovered what, at the time, were the most ancient human remains on record. The skeleton was named Lucy, after The Beatles' song 'Lucy in the Sky with Diamonds', and would later be dated as about 3.2 million years old.

Since then, genetic studies of humans and chimpanzees have suggested that we may have split from other apes much earlier than Lucy, perhaps as far as seven million years ago. Reflecting on this, we are reminded that our lives are just momentary blips in the story of human evolution, and that our time on this planet is limited.

Some of us live with the sense that time is vast and the end is far, while others live with an urgency and acute awareness of the inherent fragility and fleeting nature of life. In his powerful book *The Denial of Death*, Ernest Becker highlights the transience of the human condition: 'Man is literally split in two: he has an awareness of his own splendid uniqueness in that he sticks out of nature with a towering majesty, and yet he goes back into the ground and disappears forever.'

During our relatively short time on this earth, we spend a lot of our valuable energy in pursuit of happiness. Unfortunately, we often look in all the wrong places, searching outwards instead of recognising that the source of genuine happiness is more deeply related to the state of our own minds. There are so many examples of those who have lives of luxury and 'success', but who are miserable and depressed. Once we have our essential needs met, it's not actually the external events in our lives that determine our happiness, but rather how we relate to those events. In the words of novelist Anaïs Nin, 'We don't see things as they are, we see them as we are.' For us, one thing is certain: ultimately we can't control everything that happens to us. However, we have the ability to develop our minds in a way that supports us in meeting the many challenges of being human with resilience, wisdom and ease.

As humans, we've been gifted with a limitless capacity for growth and transformation through the powerful technology inside our heads, which, supported by the right training, can be an engine driving us towards enduring happiness and wellbeing. It is the very nature of our brains to be continuously sculpted by experiences, and science clearly demonstrates that what we regularly practise gets reinforced through the brain's exquisite capacity to adapt and reconfigure itself. However, the form that adaptation takes depends on what exactly it *is* that we are practising. When we practise worrying, the worrying circuits of the brain are reinforced. When we practise gratitude, the brain becomes more capable of noticing the good in our lives. When we practise mindfulness meditation, it forms new neural pathways that support focus, calm and emotional balance.

Just as we learn how to drive a car, mindfulness meditation teaches us how to steer our own minds and move through our lives without falling into unnecessary mental potholes. Throughout this one-month program and beyond, by maintaining a regular mindfulness practice using the different meditations offered in *The Happiness Plan*, your brain will be developing in ways that support improved attention and greater happiness. You will become a master of your mind rather than a slave to it, which is an essential ingredient in developing a happier, more fulfilling life. As you build a wiser and more compassionate relationship with yourself, the way you relate to others will similarly transform as you discover increased patience, more forgiveness and less reactivity in your relationships.

By making space to regularly pause, connect with ourselves and discover the nature of our own minds, we also become clearer about the things that really matter to us – the things that we most value in our lives. It takes great effort to resist the hyperconnected-yet-disconnected, increasingly busy way of our modern world, especially with the tentacles of technology constantly pulling at our attention. As an antidote to this, we need a regular practice that anchors us back to ourselves, and helps us develop the qualities that support our genuine happiness in these demanding times.

Over this last month, through practising the daily meditations and mindfulness exercises in this book, you have invested in developing inner resources that will support you for the rest of your life. Although you may have picked up this book seeking personal happiness, you'll also very likely discover – as I did – that the happier we are within ourselves, the more we can be of service to others in the world. As we contribute more to others, there is a positive impact on our own wellbeing, so it becomes a positive cycle towards happiness. When we train our minds through mindfulness meditation, we start to access a sense of connection to all of humanity, and to the aliveness of our planet. In the words of naturalist John Muir, 'When one tugs at a single thing in nature, he finds it attached to the rest of the world.' This 'turning inwards' is an essential ingredient for not only solving our biggest personal challenges and experiencing greater happiness, but raising our collective awareness and wisdom, and positively transforming our world.

Which brings us back to Lucy. Human beings have survived and evolved throughout millennia, and perhaps our most extraordinary survival skill is the brain's capacity to adapt and transform in relation to its environment. Just as a few million years ago, the ability to use tools allowed humans to evolve into a more sophisticated version of themselves. It raises the possibility that with our current scientific understanding of the brain, we may be able to initiate another evolutionary upgrade for our species. These insights into the long history of the human race can also inspire us to reflect on our mortality and purpose. They lead us to consider how we can make our relatively short time on this earth more meaningful, so that when we arrive at the end, we can feel our lives were well lived.

We don't often pause long enough to consider these questions until we are stopped in our tracks and forced to do so – often in situations such as unexpected medical diagnoses or the death of a loved one, moments that bring an acute sense of the fragility of life.

The challenge is to find a way to remain awake to life without these tragic wake-up calls.

For me, working as a doctor in such close relationship with illness and dying gave me a heightened sense of the preciousness of life. In some ways it was a deep lesson in mindfulness. It reminded me to appreciate the simple moments. Perhaps the most poignant experience was the time I worked in a palliative care ward. It was devastating to witness the suffering of fellow humans through the dying process, but at the same time I felt privileged to be with people as they did the work of making sense of their lives and coming to terms with their own mortality.

Working on that ward amplified my own sense of aliveness and deepened my gratitude for the simplest day-to-day experiences. At the end of each day, I'd walk across the road to the neighbouring park, particularly sensitive to the aliveness and beauty of nature. To simply see the colours of the sunset, smell the earth, hear the birds chirping, breathe effortlessly, and feel the warmth of a balmy summer night breeze across my face, filled every cell of my body with gratitude.

Mindfulness offers us this kind of larger perspective when we're not faced with death or illness – reminding us to pause and be fully present when our lives are running along their usual hectic pace. It brings us into a deep appreciation of the preciousness of our moments and the fleeting nature of it all. Each day when we practise, we remember that life is always changing, and that rather than race ahead into the next moment, we can take a breath and experience the fullness of this one. When we are in the midst of difficult times, mindfulness gives us an anchor to stay present, rather than be caught in worry or catastrophic thinking, which only amplify our suffering.

By pausing and turning inwards in meditation, we connect with a deep source of wisdom, inner strength and ease, and become more present to the miracle of all that exists around us and within us. It is this expanded awareness, clarity and resilience that becomes the foundation for our lasting happiness.

That sounds like a good plan ... don't you agree?

APPENDIX

Mindful meal

The end of this week is a great opportunity to try sharing a mindful experience with friends or family (or both). The shared meal, a ritual of gathering and bonding that has existed across all cultures and throughout history, is a good space to practise mindfulness in a group, providing a unique opportunity for deeper and more authentic connection.

Below is a suggested format you can use if you wish to host a Mindful Meal with friends, friends-to-be or family. You can cook the meal yourself, or invite the guests to bring along something to share. Take this format purely as a guideline: every group dynamic is different, and you will know what those around you find interesting, what they are comfortable with, and what they are likely to resist. For some groups, it might be enough just to have a chance to speak openly and be listened to. Other groups might enjoy sharing personal poems or be interested in long periods of meditation. Be open to the input of your guests, and allow yourself the freedom to adjust the plan as you go along.

A mindfulness practice is often a very personal and solitary one, so remember that some guests – and you might be one of them – may feel embarrassed or awkward about revealing this part of themselves to a group. Many of us cringe at the thought of appearing overly earnest or vulnerable in front of others. Approaching the process with a light-hearted, playful attitude is one way to ease those anxieties.

Purpose

Facilitate deeper and more authentic connections with one another. Allow time and space to get together with friends and like-minded people over food and conversation.

Benefits

- Space and time for meditation and shared practice.
- A deeper appreciation of food and a healthier way of eating.
- Fulfilment through real connection.
- A space for creativity and meetings of like-minded people.

Process

1. Mindful Meditation (10–30min). Decide on the length of your meditation depending on the needs and setting of the group. You could play a guided meditation or sit in silence with a timer. It may be a shorter practice to set the mood, or as you become more experienced you may increase the duration.

2. Mindful Mouthfuls (45min). Everyone brings a plate to share (decide beforehand on dietary requirements). If some guests are new to mindfulness, the host can read from these guidelines about the purpose and process of Mindful Meals. This will prepare them to be more mindful while eating and sharing conversation.

3. Mindful Mingling (30-45min). Opportunity to share and reflect from the heart. This can be in a circle, or shared

more casually during the meal, while guests practise mindful listening. Make your own meaningful questions, or reflect on the ones below. Each guest can take a turn to reflect on these topics, while others bring mindful attention to the speaker. If you feel inspired, add a dash of poetry to the night. Find a poem that inspires you and read it to the group.

Some questions you can mindfully contemplate with the group during your mindful meal:

- What makes you feel most alive in life?
- What gives your life most meaning?
- Can you share a story about a moment in your life that you especially appreciate?
- What is one thing you are most proud of in your life so far?
- If this circle could infuse you with a quality you need more of in your life at the moment, what would it be and how would you use it?
- What are three things you are most grateful for right now?
- What are three books that have taught you something that has had a tangible impact on your life?

Some recommended poets for inspiration:

- Rumi
- Hafiz
- David Whyte
- Mary Oliver

THANKS

It takes a village to raise a child and a tribe to write a book.

To my daughter, Anoushka, may you be happy and have a life that is deeply aligned with your inner spark. You are a source of light and delight, and you are also the greatest spiritual teacher I have encountered, showing me exactly how I need to grow. I hope you benefit from my own learning and develop the self-compassion and self-trust that are crucial for a flourishing life.

To my mother, Mooky, words cannot express the gratitude I feel towards you. You introduced me to meditation and your bookshelf was always a wonderland of ideas and learning. Your generosity, love and deep wisdom, along with our shared interest in spirituality and the human experience, has profoundly enriched my life. Thank you for your support in bouncing around ideas, coming on the journey, and being the most wonderful grandmother as well as mother, supporting me to do this work in the world alongside raising a child. What good karma I must have had to land in your sphere!

To my father, John, and to my brother, Anton, your adventurous spirit, courage and determination are contagious and inspire me with the energy needed to 'climb any mountain'.

To my partner, Ford, your playful spirit and optimism keep me balanced and your willingness to grow and learn, is something I deeply value. You're a crucial ingredient to my own 'Happiness Plan' and I'm so grateful for your love, care, creativity and strength. To Ron, Shirley and Nikki, thanks for your generosity and for understanding when my head is buried in a project.

To the book tribe. To Dina Kluska, thank you for catalysing this process. To the team at Affirm Press, thank you for supporting me along the road to bringing this book to life, special mention to Ruby Ashby-Orr for editing and generally keeping me on track. To Maegan Brown, you're an angel. To my aunty Nuritt Borsky, thank you so much for your advice and time spent reviewing the manuscript. To Katia Ariel and Sue Auster, your feedback was greatly appreciated.

To Sun Hyland, (www.newearthcatering.com/loving-good-food) thank you for your magnificent recipes and music, which have nourished me many times over. To Amy Crawford (www.theholisticingredient. com), thank you for your creative recipes, generosity, friendship and sense of humour. To my dearest, wise friends who have supported me along this project and many others. You know who you are, and my life is greatly enriched with you in it.

To my meditation teachers – I'm so grateful for your generosity, wisdom and compassion. It's reassuring to know such human beings exist in this world.

Finally, to you, the Mindful in May community, thank you for being part of this global movement towards greater good in the world, and for generously contributing to saving the lives of thousands through the gift of clean water.

REFERENCES

(Page 4) *... one of Davidson's studies revealed that just seven hours of compassion meditation over a two-week period resulted in measurable changes in the brain, and also had a positive impact on behaviour ...*

Lutz, A., Brefcynski-Lewis, J., Johnstone, T., & Davidson, R. J. (2008). Regulation of the neural circuitry of emotion by compassion meditation: Effects of meditative expertise. *PLoS ONE,* 3(3). https://doi.org/10.1371/journal. pone.0001897

(Page 4) *Merzenich and his team demonstrated that regular brain training not only allowed their brains to continue growing and maintain function into old age, but could actually reverse age-related functional decline.*

de Villers-Sidani, E., Alzghoul, L., Zhou, X., Simpson, K. L., Lin, R. C., & Merzenich, M. M. (2010). Recovery of functional and structural age-related changes in the rat primary auditory cortex with operant training. *Proceedings of the National Academy of Sciences,* 107(31), 13900–13905. doi:10.1073/pnas.1007885107

(Page 7) *A group of psychologists in England named Mark Williams, John Teasdale and Zindel Segal conducted a study of patients who had suffered multiple episodes of depression.*

Williams, M., Teasdale, J., Segal, Z., Kabat-Zinn, J. (2007). *The Mindful Way Through Depression.* New York: Guilford Publications.

(Page 10) *Resistance can show up in many forms and often it's through self-criticism or self-doubt ...*

Pressfield, S. (2012). *The War of Art: Winning the Inner Creative Battle.* USA: Black Irish Entertainment

(Page 13) *found that patients suffering from psoriasis (a chronic skin condition) who participated in mindfulness programs healed more rapidly ...*

Kabat-Zinn, J., Wheeler, E., Light, T., Skillings, A., Scharf, M. J., Cropley, T. G., & Bernhard, J. D. (1998). Influence of a mindfulness meditation-based stress reduction intervention on rates of skin clearing in patients with moderate to severe psoriasis undergoing photo therapy (UVB) and photochemotherapy (PUVA). *Psychosomatic Medicine,* 60(5), 625-632. Retrieved from https://www.ncbi.nlm.nih.gov/pubmed

(Page 14) *... forty per cent of our potential happiness is within our control and determined by 'what we do in our daily lives and how we think'.*

Lyubomirsky, S. (2010). *The How of Happiness: A New Approach to Getting the Life You Want.* Sydney: Hachette.

(Page 14) *... Richard Davidson demonstrated that just one day of mindfulness practice could reduce the expression of specific genes associated with inflammation in the body ...*

Kaliman, P., Álvarez-López, M. J., Cosín-Tomás, M., Rosenkranz, M. A., Lutz, A., & Davidson, R. J. (2014). Rapid changes in histone deacetylases and inflammatory gene expression in expert meditators. *Psychoneuroendocrinology,* 40, 96-107. https://doi.org/10.1016/j. psyneuen.2013.11.004

(Page 15) *With the World Health Organisation (WHO) announcing that depression has become the leading cause of ill health and disability ...*

World Health Organisation. (2017) 'Depression: let's talk' says WHO, as depression tops list of causes of ill health. Media Centre World Health Organisation. Retrieved from http://www.who.int/mediacentre/news/releases/2017/world-health-day/en/

(Page 18) *In a famous study, Daniel Gilbert, an American psychologist, wanted to investigate just how distracted our minds actually are …*

Killingsworth, M. A., & Gilbert, D. T. (2010). A wandering mind is an unhappy mind. *Science*, 330(6006), 932-932. Retrieved from http://science. sciencemag.org

(Page 19) I*n 1863, Russian novelist and philosopher Fyodor Dostoyevsky was considering the problem …*

Dostoyevsky, F. (1985). *Winter notes on summer impressions.* (FitzLyon, K. Trans.) London: Quartet. (Original work published 1955). Retrieved from http://openlibrary.org/books/OL15248986M

(Page 20) *Davidson's research in this area demonstrated that people who meditated for a minimum of thirty hours over a two-month period had less active amygdalas.*

Davidson, R & Begley, S. (2012) *The Emotional Life of Your Brain: How Its Unique Patterns Affect the Way You Think, Feel, and Live – and How You Can Change Them.* Melbourne: Penguin Random House.

(page 22) *In the book* The Science of Meditation, *Daniel Goleman explains: 'No brain lab had ever before seen gamma oscillations that persist for minutes rather than split seconds, are so strong, and are in synchrony across widespread regions of the brain …'*

Goleman, D. (2017). *The Science of Meditation.* Melbourne: Penguin Random House.

(Page 62) *How was it possible, I asked myself, to walk for an hour through the woods and see nothing worthy of note?*

Keller, H. (1933). Three Days to See. *Atlantic Monthly.* Retrieved from http:// www.afb.org

(Page 68) *Kristin Neff defines self-compassion as having three components …*

Neff, N. (n.d). The Three Elements of Self-Compassion. *Self-Compassion.* Retrieved from http://self-compassion.org/the-three-elements-of-self-compassion-2/

(Page 69) *Research has demonstrated that people who have greater self-compassion experience less depression and anxiety, and greater happiness and life satisfaction.*

Neff, K. D. (2011). Self-compassion, self-esteem, and well-being. *Social and Personality Psychology Compass*, 5(1), 1-12. http://dx.doi.org/10.1111/j.1751-9004.2010.00330.x

(Page 71) *Recent research has identified the literal 'brain in your gut'.*

Mayer, E. A. (2011). Gut feelings: The emerging biology of gut–brain communication. *Nature Reviews Neuroscience*, 12(8), 453-466. doi:10.1038/nrn3071

(Page 85) *After eight weeks of meditation, the amygdala, the stress centre of the brain, was reduced in volume, which implied a reduction in its activity.*

Hölzel, B. K., Carmody, J., Evans, K. C., Hoge, E. A., Dusek, J. A., Morgan, L., & Lazar, S. W. (2009). Stress reduction correlates with structural changes in the amygdala. *Social Cognitive and Affective Neuroscience*, 5(1), 11-17. Retrieved from https://www.ncbi.nlm.nih.gov/pmc

(Page 97) *Multi-tasking has been demonstrated to reduce brain density in areas that control empathy and emotions (the anterior cingulate cortex).*

Loh, K. K., & Kanai, R. (2014). Higher media multi-tasking activity is associated with smaller gray-matter density in the anterior cingulate cortex. *PLoS ONE*, 9(9), https://doi.org/10.1371/journal.pone.0106698

(Page 97) *A study at the University of London found that subjects who multi-tasked experienced drops in their IQ comparable to someone who missed a night of sleep.*

Gillespie, I. (2015). Multitasking makes you stupid, studies find. *The Sydney Morning Herald*. Retrieved from http://www.smh.com.au/digital-life/digital-life-news/multitasking-makes-you-stupid-studies-find-20150520-gh5ouq.html

(Page 97) *A famous study at Stanford led by Clifford Nass, revealed that multi-taskers were not as effective at remembering and learning new information.*

Ophir, E., Nass, C., & Wagner, A. D. (2009). Cognitive control in media multitaskers. *Proceedings of the National Academy of Sciences*, 106(37), 15583-15587. doi:10.1073/pnas.0903620106

(**Page 99**) *The Pomodoro Technique was created in the 1980s by Francesco Cirillo, and it involves dividing your work time into twenty-five-minute increments of focused attention with regular breaks in between.*

Cirillo, F. (2006). The Pomodoro Technique (the pomodoro). Retrieved from http://www.baomee.info/pdf/technique/1.pdf

(**Page 101**) *Linda Stone, a technology thought leader and ex-Microsoft researcher discovered a condition she described as 'email apnoea' ...*

Stone, L. (2014). Are you breathing? Do you have email apnea?. *Linda Stone.* Retrieved from https://lindastone.net/2014/11/24/are-you-breathing-do-you-have-email-apnea/

(**page 101**) *Craig Palsson, professor of economics at Yale University, investigated whether there was a link between the two ...*

Palsson, C. (2014). That Smarts!: Smartphones and child injuries. *Department of Economics, Yale.* Retrieved from http://www.palssonresearch.org/wp-content/uploads/2014/10/smartphone_v17.pdf

(**page 125**) '*I remember one morning when I discovered a cocoon in the back of a tree just as a butterfly was making a hole in its case and preparing to come out ...*'

Kazanzakis, N. (2000). *Zorba the Greek.* (Wildman, C. Trans.). London: Faber. (Original work published 1952)

(**Page 154**) *Paul Ekman, psychologist and emotion guru, discovered seven universal basic emotions experienced by people in all cultures ...*

Ekman, P. (n.d). Micro Expressions. *Paul Ekman Group.* Retrieved from https://www.paulekman.com/micro-expressions/

(**Page 155**) *Even more interestingly, he notes that it's possible to experience an emotion by first activating the facial muscles involved in that particular emotion.*

Levenson, R. W., Ekman, P., & Friesen, W. V. (1990). Voluntary facial action generates emotion-specific autonomic nervous system activity. *Psychophysiology*, 27(4), 363-384. doi:10.1111/j.1469-8986.1990.tb02330.x

(Page 157) *In his book,* The Yes Brain, *Psychiatrist and mindfulness expert Daniel Siegel shares a powerful metaphor for how we can gain greater emotional balance and resilience.*

Siegel, D. J., & Payne Bryson, T. (2018). *The Yes Brain.* New York: Bantam Dell Publishing Group, Div of Random House, Inc.

(page 168) *According to Daniel Goleman, our basal ganglia stores information about everything we do and keeps track of our decisions …*

Goleman, D. (2015). With the new year comes an opportunity to reboot our habits – Drop the negative ones and start better ones. *Daniel Goleman.* Retrieved from http://www.danielgoleman.info/daniel-goleman-3-secrets-to-habit-change/

(page 169) *'Carl Jung describes visiting Taos, New Mexico, to learn about Native American culture'*

Gung, C. G. (1989). *Memories, dreams, reflections.* (Winston R., & Winston C. Trans.) New York: Vintage Books. (Original work published 1962)

(Page 174) *He shared details of his confinement with journalist Gregory Warner on the podcast Rough Translation.*

NPR. (2017, Sep 11). How 'Anna Karenina' saved a Somali inmate's life [Audio podcast]. *Rough Translation.* Retrieved from https://www.npr.org/2017/09/11/550058353/rough-translation-how-anna-karenina-saved-a-somali-inmates-life

(Page 175) *One of the longest-running studies of human development, called the Grant study, looked at a group of 268 male students from Harvard.*

Mineo, L. (1938). Good genes are nice, but joy is better. *The Harvard Gazette.* https://news.harvard.edu/gazette/story/2017/04/over-nearly-80-years-harvard-study-has-been-showing-how-to-live-a-healthy-and-happy-life/

REFERENCES

(Page 197) *Gil Fronsdal, an American meditation teacher, compares being lost in one of the obstacles to wandering through a maze with your eyes on the ground ...*

Fronsdal, Gill. (n.d). The Hinderence of restlesness and worry [Adapted talk]. *Insight Meditation center.* http://www.insightmeditationcenter.org/books-articles/articles/the-five-hindrances-handouts/the-hindrance-of-restlessness-worry/

(Page 230) *A study by Rachel and Stephen Kaplan revealed that 'office workers with a view of nature liked their jobs more, enjoyed better health and reported greater life satisfaction'.*

Kaplan, R., & Kaplan, S. (1989). *The experience of nature: A psychological perspective.* Cambridge: Cambridge University Press. Retrieved from https://openlibrary.org/books/OL2053637M/The_experience_of_nature

(Page 230) *Roger S Ulrich, director of the Center for Health Systems and Design at Texas A&M University, conducted a famous study which found that nature can help the body heal.*

Ulrich, R. S. (1984). View through a window may influence recovery from surgery. *Science, 224*(4647), 420-421. doi:10.1126/science.6143402

(Page 230) *David Strayer, cognitive psychologist at the University of Utah, demonstrated that after three days of wilderness backpacking ...*

Atchley, R. A., Strayer, D. L., & Atchley, P. (2012). Creativity in the wild: Improving creative reasoning through immersion in natural settings. *PloS ONE, 7*(12). https://doi.org/10.1371/journal.pone.0051474

(page 230) *Finally, a Stanford-led study has found that walking in nature could lower the risk of depression.*

Bratman, G. N., Hamilton, J. P., Hahn, K. S., Daily, G. C., & Gross, J. J. (2015). Nature experience reduces rumination and subgenual prefrontal cortex activation. *Proceedings of the National Academy of Sciences, 112*(28), 8567-8572. doi:10.1073/pnas.1510459112

(Page 242) *A study by Dr Joshua Brown, professor of psychological brain sciences at Indiana University, looked at the benefits of gratitude for three hundred students*

Kini, P., Wong, J., McInnis, S., Gabana, N., & Brown, J. W. (2016). The effects of gratitude expression on neural activity. *NeuroImage*, 128, 1-10. https://doi.org/10.1016/j.neuroimage.2015.12.040

(Page 242) *Gratitude is also a powerful antidote to toxic emotions. Robert Emmons, one of the world's leading gratitude researchers, demonstrated that regular gratitude reduced feelings of envy and resentment*

Emmons, R. A., & McCullough, M. E. (2003). Counting blessings versus burdens: An experimental investigation of gratitude and subjective well-being in daily life. *Journal of Personality and Social Psychology*, 84(2), 377. http://dx.doi.org/10.1037/0022-3514.84.2.377

(Page 244) *Research by Martin Seligman, pioneer of the positive psychology movement, demonstrates that people who write a letter to someone they appreciate increase their own levels of happiness*

Seligman, M. E. (2011). *Flourish: A visionary new understanding of happiness and well-being.* New York: Atria.